Basic Bush Survival

Basic Bush Survival

E. C. (Ted) Meyers

hancock
house

ISBN 0-88839-399-7
Copyright © 1997 E. C. (Ted) Meyers

Cataloging in Publication Data
Meyers, Edward C.

Basic bush survival

ISBN 0-88839-399-7

1. Wilderness survival. I. Basic bush survival.
GV200.5.M49 1997   613.6'9   C97-910097-6

Printed in Hong Kong—Colorcraft

Editor: Nancy Miller
Production: Sharon Boglari
Cover design: Andrew Jaster

Published simultaneously in Canada and the United States by

HANCOCK HOUSE PUBLISHERS LTD.
19313 Zero Avenue, Surrey, BC V4P 1M7
(604) 538-1114   Fax (604) 538-2262

HANCOCK HOUSE PUBLISHERS
1431 Harrison Avenue, Blaine, WA 98230-5005
(604) 538-1114   Fax (604) 538-2262

Contents

Dedication

To the memory of Fred Henderson (1874-1954).
No one knew the northern woods better or loved them more.

Acknowledgments

Many thanks to the research staff in the photo section of the National Archives, Ottawa.

Also by E. C. Meyers:

Thunder in the Morning Calm: The R.C.N. in Korea, 1950-1955
Children of the Thunderbird: Legend and Myths of the West Coast

Introduction

This book is not intended for the experienced hikers or woodsmen who know what they are doing in the bush. Neither is it intended for serious plant gatherers, as they are well acquainted with the plants they seek. They have already studied the excellent books which have been written on the subject, books which teach the serious student of wood lore and herb gathering not only how to identify thousands of plants but also how to use them as food and medicine. This book has a totally different purpose. It is a sort of Wilderness 101, if you will, and is intended for those who do not realize the bush is a good place to avoid unless you know a thing or two about it. Still, while it can be hostile, dangerous and inhospitable, there is no reason to think of the wilderness as being so fearsome that it cannot be tamed.

Most people who become lost in the bush find themselves in trouble because they go in oblivious to the dangers, sometimes on purpose but more often by accident. Most of these people find themselves in deep trouble because they fail to take a few simple precautions. This book will help you avoid, or at least alleviate, much of the danger you will encounter.

Every year in Canada and the United States, hundreds of hikers, hunters and just plain folk get lost in the woods. Most of these people are rescued, some relatively quickly. Some, however, are never found or are found dead or close to it. Some of the deaths are from starvation because the lost ones do not know they are surrounded by edible plants which they could not identify in any case.

Most other deaths are from exposure because these people do not make a shelter. Indeed, most don't know how. Only on a rare occasion does someone die because he or she falls into a chasm or is drowned in a torrential creek. Even more rarely is someone killed by an animal or because they are bitten by a poisonous snake or spider.

Some die because, in their bid to stay alive, they eat berries not knowing they are poisonous. When dealing with wild plants it is important to know whether a plant is edible, and if it is, which is the edible part. Some people perish because they drink water from alkaline water holes—just because water looks fresh, it does not automatically make it so. The saddest thing about these calamitous deaths is that most are avoidable.

Anyone, including children of reasonable age, can survive in the North American wilderness—even if a rescue is not effected for months. Not only is survival possible, one can actually live in a modicum of comfort—for months if need be. The priorities of survival—and they are simple in the extreme—can be easily memorized in three short words: **what, when** and **how**. To be successful the survivor should know what to do, when to do it and how to do it.

Most of those who perish in the bush are victims of circumstances, often aiding and abetting their unfortunate situation through ignorance, carelessness, panic, naivete and fear of the unknown. Some of those who survive do so through nothing more than sheer dumb luck or a chance sighting by a sharp-eyed searcher. Luck and chance are not good things to rely on exclusively.

The problems which arise from being lost are usually distressing, but there is no need to die because of them. This little book will show anyone who can read (or listen while someone else reads it aloud) and remember a few basic tips about ways to survive in any situation in any area of North America—including the Arctic.

Because survival is not a exact science, techniques are not cut and dried. Therefore, specific chapters deal with specific situations. Each will cover the circumstances a lost person is most likely to encounter in the hostile and unfamiliar environment into which he or she is thrust.

In addition to pictures of easily identified edible plants, berries and vegetables, there are also a few pictures of those plants, berries and vegetables which must be avoided. These include certain plants and berries which, while not fatally poison, will cause severe discomfort such as rashes, stomach and bowel upsets.

In most cases I have included the plant's scientific name although the average survivor will be little interested in such things. They are included only to aid identification of plants which may go under a variety of local names. Others are more identifiable when there is only one generic name (a dandelion, blueberry or cattail goes by the same name in the U.S. as it does in Canada).

Specific plants having edible parts, even though the rest of the plant is deadly, are classified as poisonous. All plants classed poisonous, including those which are not fatal but cause rashes and temporary discomforts, are marked with a ★P. This may seem overly dramatic but it helps drive home an important point—leave it be.

Chapter 8 includes a small number of common plants which will supply the survivor with basic medicines. These are generally made into teas or syrups because tea is very easy to make and syrup is easy to swallow. As with all medicines, those from wild plants produce reactions if taken in excess. However, overdoses are rare because herbal medicines usually have a less-than-appealing flavor. Herbal tea, while good for you, at best usually tastes only so-so while herbal syrup, though an excellent medicine, usually tastes so unpleasant that you would never yearn for a second dose.

All medicinal herbs mentioned are described in detail for identification. The book goes over how to prepare them, what they can be used for and what the side-effects, if any, might be.

Do not attempt to find every plant listed. Such a venture is not only unnecessary, it cannot be done because certain plants inhabit certain areas. All you should do is locate three or four of the listed species, be certain of identification and then depend on them exclusively. In other words, utilize what is readily available and do not concern yourself with any others.

Chapter 11 deals specifically with snares and traps for animals, large and small. The book covers how to properly make, rig and set the traps, how to prepare and cook the animals caught and how to utilize the fur, bones and sinews. The part of the chapter dealing with small animals is for those who are not rescued within seven days while the part dealing with large animals is strictly for those who are still in the bush, after three weeks with little hope in sight.

If it becomes your unhappy lot to spend more than a week in the bush you are going to have to find meat and fish for protein as few plants contain enough of that important nutrient. Again, do not concern yourself with attaining great variety. If rabbits are plentiful—snare rabbits. If squirrels are in abundance—snare squirrels. Live on what is available and don't bother trying to find something that may not even be in the area. You will be wasting your time, and time in the bush is valuable.

Besides snares you will be shown how to make a fish net and a night line as well as the best bait. Also shown is the proper way to tie a line to a hook. (Don't chuckle so knowingly. Very few survivors know that improperly tied lines catch nothing but weeds, snag and break the line or unravel and drop the hooks. You cannot afford to lose anything as valuable as a hook.) A properly tied hook performs the action for which it is intended. Meaning, as the hook rides the currents it gets the best motion out of the bait thus attracting fish, which is the primary intention.

The best part of the learned art of survival is that it doesn't require a great deal of equipment. Anyone who goes hiking, hunting, canoeing or boating in unfamiliar territory should carry a few basic items. This applies equally to those who fly in small planes across heavily wooded areas. These needs are all described in Chapter 3.

If you become lost and don't have anything but the clothes on your back, the task of survival will become extremely difficult but certainly not impossible. That situation, a worst-case scenario, is covered in Chapter 16.

Therefore, if you or someone you know might be venturing into the bush anytime in the future, flying over rugged country or trail riding without a qualified guide (guides have been known to get lost as well) through unfamiliar terrain, check out this book first. Make it part of your basic kit or give it to your friends as part of their kits. It could prove to be your salvation, perhaps your only friend, for a greater number of days than you care to think about. If you do use it, and it helps you pull through, drop me a line in care of the publisher. I would like to hear of your experiences. Perhaps you might discover something new that can be passed on for use by others.

E. C. MEYERS

1 Learn the Basic Rules

Some years ago two hikers on an early winter backpack trip in a heavily wooded area of the Kootenay Valley discovered the wreckage of a single-engine aircraft. Although heavily damaged in the crash, it had not burned. What remained of the pilot was found under a jagged outcrop of rock about 200 yards from the plane.

Investigators determined that the wreckage was fifty miles north of the original flight plan; the pilot had lived several weeks before dying of exposure and hunger, although he had survived the crash with only a broken ankle; that he had left the plane, possibly fearing it was about to catch fire, and he had hobbled to the rocky shelter. There, because he knew a search would be launched and anticipating rescue, he lit a small fire and sat back. Rescue never came. As is customary, after seven days, because nothing was found, the search had been scaled back and then eventually called off.

Unfortunately, the pilot had done nothing in the way of basic survival beyond lighting a fire and eating a bag of cookies he had with him, a supply which could not have lasted more than a day or two.

A small stream flowed nearby which would have supplied him with plenty of water for drinking and in which to boil the cattails and water-lily tubers which abounded near the banks. He had not caught any of the fish which were present in abundance. He had also failed to recognize the presence of animals and edible vegetation which surrounded him. The cattails alone would have kept him alive for months.

The pilot had been found dressed in the suit he had worn when he left on his flight and a raincoat with which he had tried to stave off the chill of the mountain nights. He had attempted to set his ankle but had done such a poor job that it began an imperfect knit which would make walking extremely painful. He had bound the ankle with material from the plane's first-aid kit, but had never rebound it, possibly because it had become too painful to touch.

An empty aspirin container from the plane's first-aid kit was mute evidence that the ankle had troubled him greatly especially after he had used the last tablet. Yet, he was only a few feet from a grove of white willow trees, a natural source of aspirin. But he did not know it.

A search of the wreckage determined he had failed to utilize any parts of the plane as aids to basic survival. He should have known he had much at his disposal. The fuel tanks, which had not ruptured, contained gasoline which he could have used. Control wires remained intact. A length of nylon rope, still coiled, lay unused in a storage compartment. The fabric of the aircraft seats, the headlining, the instrument panel, all useful survival aids, had not been utilized.

The pilot died a lonely, needless death from hunger and exposure, probably in great pain from his injured ankle. Could he have avoided his fate? The answer is: in all likelihood, yes. All he had to do was follow a few basic rules.

The first rule was the most important. Injuries are the first things that **must** be attended to. Superficial wounds, minor sprains, abrasions and bruises can wait, but severe sprains, broken bones and deep, bleeding cuts have to be looked after at once. (First aid is covered in Chapter 18.) The pilot's fate might well have been different had he known the rules of basic survival.

The Anagram that Means Survival

The words BASIC SURVIVAL are an anagram representing five items of common sense and seven rules.

First, the common sense:

Be prepared
Anticipate
Speculate
Improvise where necessary
Come to grips with the situation

Second, the seven rules:

Shelter is the primary concern
Utilize everything that can be used
Reconnoiter to learn the terrain
Vary your daily routine
Itemize, list and know your equipment
Verify (if possible) your location
Allocate and use your supplies properly
Logic must be used always

The seven rules apply to all areas of the continent and should be followed faithfully. If there is a single-most important rule it is logic. If you are to survive, you must think continuously, and when you are lost you must consider all things carefully. You must make the correct decisions, for only rarely will there be time for a second chance.

One of your first decisions is to admit to yourself that you are lost. Many go into a period of denial. This **must** be avoided. Don't sit around waiting for someone to rescue you. Rescue is highly unlikely for the time being.

Secondly, you must realize that you are an extremely tiny speck on an immensely vast spread of land. Remind yourself that North America is a land mass exceeding 9 million square miles in area and you are standing on about nine square feet of it. In other words, you are the proverbial stalk of wheat in the field. From the air you will be as hard to see as that stalk of wheat and you will be no less easy to see at ground level.

Thirdly, you must admit to yourself that you, alone, are responsible for your immediate well-being. No one is likely to miraculously appear to relieve you of that problem. Once you make those admissions and push denial out of the way, your task will become somewhat easier.

Shelter—the primary concern

The moment you realize you are lost it is imperative that your thoughts turn to shelter. There is never time to waste as a shelter must be completed before darkness settles. That task will be either simple or difficult depending on where you are and what you have to work with. Building a shelter in a forest is obviously much easier than making one in a desert or in the Arctic; but, regardless of where you are, shelter is your first concern.

The reasons for this should be obvious. You have no guarantee that rescue will come quickly. In fact, quick rescues are almost unheard of. Therefore, if you are wise you will become a pessimist because a pessimist will anticipate a long stay. This is not to say you should abandon hope. Simply admit to yourself that your stay in the bush may be longer than you would wish. You **must** build a shelter.

A shelter provides many things besides being a dry, relatively safe place to sleep. One of your main concerns, particularly in the mountains and northern forests, must be of animals, mosquitos, hornets, wasps and other annoying insects. A shelter will help you avoid them. It will give you respite from the sun, from the cold and, particularly in winter, will keep you out of the wind. You should be aware that most winter deaths are caused by frigid winds rather than frigid temperatures. The shelter will help deal with all these adversities, plus—and this is very important—it is also a place for storage.

In wooded areas, the best shelter is a simple lean-to made of trees and leafy or needled branches. Needled branches are always best as they provide compact layers. In the Arctic, the ice in winter and the tundra in summer is all you will have for building materials. There is nothing else. In areas of open plains you can make a good shelter from sod. In rocky areas, stones should be used.

Utilize everything

Everything means exactly that—everything. Even a short length of string or an elastic band may prove useful. Throw nothing away. Keep even the silver paper from your candy bars. When attached to poles, it can be used as a reflector. If you are the victim of a plane crash, salvage everything useful from the plane. The plane can provide temporary shelter but extreme care must be taken because of trapped oil and the gas in the tanks. Also, a metal plane will conduct cold as well as heat. In winter you will actually be better off in a well-built lean-to with a small fire at the opening than inside the metal shell of a plane where a fire must **never** be built.

If you are lucky enough to have a rifle or pistol make sure you keep it in clean condition, and be very certain it is safe to use. Check the barrel for mud or other blockages before loading it. If you squeeze the trigger of a primed firearm and the barrel is plugged, even partially, you will likely be seriously injured if not killed. If the firearm is unusable, keep all the shells as they have their uses.

Tins and other containers can save your life. They can also kill you so it is necessary to know what they contained, which ones to use and in which way. Keep them though, for all have a use of some sort, if only as a minnow trap (see Chapter 11) or as a strainer to remove the tannin from acorns (see Chapter 5).

Reconnoiter the terrain

It is important to learn about your surroundings. This should be done through carefully measured walks from your base camp covering every direction. This applies to forests and heavily bushed areas where visibility is limited. Open plains, tundra and desert are all cases of what you see is what you've got. There is no point in trudging across twenty miles of sand and sagebrush or snow and tundra to the far horizon only to see another twenty miles of sand and sagebrush or snow and tundra. Stay put and concentrate on staying alive. In all likelihood, in an open space, searchers will see you long before you will see them.

Woods and forests, however, present an entirely different scenario. There your visibility will be limited to a few hundred yards or even less. No matter where you look, all you are going to see are trees and more trees. In this case it makes perfect sense to search around for the simple reason that from your campsite you are not going to see a far-off horizon.

Reconnoitering makes sense. Some years ago a friend of mine became lost on a fishing trip in the British Columbia interior when he took a wrong turn and became separated from the rest of the party. He was a seasoned veteran of the woods and, because it was late in the day, realized no one was going to find him before morning. Accepting the fact that he was alone he spent the rest of the daylight building a lean-to and preparing his campsite. He spent a safe night. The following morning he decided to look around the area—and within 300 yards came upon a logging road, saw smoke in the distance and walked two miles to a busy camp. The amused loggers returned him to his fishing camp just as a search party was preparing to leave.

Therefore, once you have tended your wounds and built your shelter, think about looking for a way out. But, not before those two primary chores have been done.

Variety

Variety, it is said, adds zest to existence. This old axiom is no less true in the bush as it is in a city. Above all, keep busy doing different things. For the most part, those who are lost do nothing; and inactivity saps not only the will to live but erodes strength as well. Many who are lost fare badly because they do exactly the same things day after day. Every two or three days start the morning with something different. Plan your days so there is some variance however small it may be. Keep a diary and record faithfully the events of each day, the animals you see and the plants you find. Mention anything out of the ordinary.

The one thing you should never vary is personal cleanliness. Many survivors are brought out of the woods looking like starved wolves and smelling like bears. This is not necessary. In fact, it is foolish. A morning wash—hot water if you can manage it—pays dividends. It keeps up morale and fires the will to keep going.

Itemize all equipment

Whether you find yourself blessed with some equipment or possess but a single knife, it makes little difference if you lose or cannot find something when you need it. Know what you have, know its condition and above all know how and when to use it. Never trim a sapling with a knife if you have a hatchet. Never use a hatchet to sharpen a fish spear if you have a knife. The last thing you need is to be hurt; and using the wrong piece of equipment is a sure way to cause injury.

List, mentally or on paper, what you have, find a safe place to keep each piece making sure to return it to its place after use. Never leave equipment on the ground; hang it from a branch or store it in the lean-to. This may seem an unimportant rule until you mislay your ax or lose your knife. Many a lost person has discovered to his or her sorrow just how easy it is for an item of importance to become covered by snow or fallen leaves. **Know what you have and where it will be when you need it**.

Verify your location

You will serve yourself well if you take some time during your first evening as a lost soul to sit under the stars and record the positions of the celestial bodies you recognize. Find the Big Dipper (*Ursa Major*) for it will direct you to the north star. Imagine a straight line is extended upwards from the two outer (right side, opposite the "handle" of the dipper) stars of the dipper. This line will point directly to the north star, the closest bright star. Identification will be easy because in the intense darkness of a forest night the north star often appears almost close enough to be within reach of an outstretched hand. To the novice, who has never looked at stars except through the haze of civilization, this can be an unsettling sensation. Place a line of stones or sticks in the shape of an arrow pointing in the direction of the north star. The following morning, because you now know where north is, you will be able to narrow the area by using the sun in conjunction with a watch (see Chapter 3).

If you know more or less where you are, you will be better able to determine your chances of being found in good time. If, on the other hand, you have no idea at all of your whereabouts you might as well prepare for a period of being well and truly alone. Passengers in aircraft fall into this category. How many passengers ever know, beyond roughly, the part of the country they are flying over? Very few.

"Where are we now, dear?"

"I think we're over Idaho. Maybe Montana."

"Someone said we were flying a northern route."

"Oh? Well, in that case we are probably over Canada somewhere."

In an aircraft, whether a huge jet or a two-seat Cessna, in all probability only the pilot is aware of location; and, while unfortunate, it is an all too accurate statistic that the pilot is often killed in the crash, taking with him the location. Even knowing you're in Idaho or B.C. or New Mexico or West Virginia is of little help if you do not know in which part of the state or province you are located. If there are more survivors than just one, the situation will differ slightly. (Groups are dealt with in Chapter 10.)

Allocate your supplies

Those who are lost must face another important truth: you are going to be hungry—at least for part of the time—and it is far better to be hungry in the beginning than later when you will need all the strength you can muster. Therefore, after you have itemized your equipment, turn to your immediately available food stocks, if you have any. Decide how far they will take you on a minimum per day diet. If, for example, you find you have a bag of twenty cookies, five packs of cocoa, a tin of Spam and one candy bar, allot it into rations for ten days. If you are going to be rescued it will likely be within that time.

Now then, the above is not very much. What it breaks down to is two cookies, half a cup of cocoa, one thin slice of Spam and one-tenth of the candy bar **each day**. That is not enough to keep you going for any length of time but, whatever you do with your available rations, do not gobble down everything within two days. As a matter of fact it is advisable **not** to eat any of your emergency food during your first day. Because of the trauma you will feel in your situation you will not be particularly hungry anyway. Failure to economize is probably the best guarantee that, if you are ever discovered, there will be very little left for the rescuers to carry out.

Therefore, you must begin to make plans to supplement your larder within the first couple of days. You must use what is around you. That means small animals, birds, roots, berries, fish if you are near a lake, stream or river and whatever else nature's bounty might provide—and nature provides a wondrous bounty if you know what to look for. You may eventually also have to consider insects. You read correctly—insects. Plump, protein-packed insects.

You must also consider that the allocation rule includes the safeguarding of what you have. Animals, large and small, not only share your new surroundings but many will be pleased, even anxious, to share your food. Some may consider you as food, so go out of your way to avoid contact with nature's larger creatures. The most dangerous animals are wolverines and bears, in that order. The worst nuisances are raccoons, the most destructive are porcupines and the most fearsome, but least dangerous, are wolves. Cougars, the wilderness' version of a wild card, are definitely to be avoided.

Remember, any wilderness animal, large or small, will happily steal your supplies if you give it half a chance. Safeguarding is dealt with in Chapter 13.

Learn the meaning of the anagram B-A-S-I-C S-U-R-V-I-V-A-L and understand the essence of BASIC and the application of SURVIVAL. This will ensure that you will be able to take full advantage of the situation.

2 There's Danger in Them Thar Hills

More people become lost on trips into bush country than anywhere else. Experienced back packers often tell about the times
they have stumbled across hikers who are dressed more for a
PTA meeting or a patio picnic than a wilderness trail. These
amateur *coureurs de bois* are the ones who get into trouble,
mostly because they don't have the foggiest notion of where they
are going, don't know how to get there and have no idea of the
dangers they are inviting upon themselves.

A tourist with time to kill decides to hike down a trail and walks
too far before realizing he has passed that unusual rock formation at
least three times. What it means, of course, is that he has been walking
in circles. Usually he is wearing cotton shorts, a baseball cap and a
T-shirt. He is wearing canvas sneakers suited only for a primary-
school gym class. If he is wearing socks they are flimsy things,
lounging around his ankles. When he sees the rocks for the fourth time
it dawns on him that he is lost—and he panics. For the next three hours
he crashes about looking for the proper trail. Inevitably, he spends the
night serving as a buffet for voracious mosquitos and cringing at every
sound he hears. Sometimes he is found the next day; sometimes he is
alone for two or more weeks.

A hike, whether intended to last one hour or three weeks, takes
planning and should never be undertaken on a whim. The hiker owes
it not only to himself but to those who risk their lives searching for
him to take a few simple precautions.

If your travels are going to take longer than one hour, plan your
route keeping in mind the terrain. Pack a kit containing the few items
necessary for survival (see Chapter 3).

Dress properly. Wear long, warm, sturdy trousers, preferably
denim or corduroy. Wear a warm shirt (flannel is best) and a bright,
plaid woolen jacket (sometimes called a Mackinaw) or a nylon jacket.
A yellow or bright orange cap is good because it can be seen from a

distance. Warm clothing will help you survive the night and give protection from bugs, nettles and branches during the day.

Boots should be leather (with laces) and should extend above the ankles. There are sound reasons for this. First, heavy-duty boots support your ankles and minimize sprains. They protect your feet from sharp rocks. They will help keep your feet dry. The laces will prove useful in a number of ways.

Equally important, high boots protect against snakes, ground spiders and, in the southwest, scorpions. Hikers should be aware that parts of North America are home to various types of poison snakes and insects (see Chapter 9).

Tell someone of responsible age where you are going, the means of travel (canoe, boat, walking), the direction of travel and how long you expect to be away. This applies to **all** trips, long or short. Don't just wave "bye-bye" to your two-year-old nephew and lurch off down the nearest trail. Inform someone who will recall the departure and at least be able to point out the trail you took.

Even if you are not anticipating an extended trek, carry a knife or hatchet with you. This will enable you to perform what is known as "blazing a trail." This is the simple exercise of slashing a short slice down the trunk of a tree. It doesn't have to be either long or deep—just the removal of a narrow layer of bark to a length of six inches is sufficient. Leave the bark dangling so it acts like a pennant. Mark a tree every hundred feet or so. Follow the marks on your way back.

If you feel guilty about slashing trees you can achieve the same purpose by tying a colored string or ribbon around a low branch every 200 feet or so. Remove the string or ribbon as you pass on the way back. Leaving it is not good because if your run across it a second time it might fool you into taking another wrong turn. Secondly, if the string or ribbon is not removed, the branch will eventually grow **around** it and over the years form an hour-glass-shaped constriction. This will interfere with the flow of sap and hinder the tree's growth. If you don't have string, ribbon, a hatchet or a knife you can snap low branches; but that causes more damage than slashes and should be used only as a last resort.

Do not make the same mistake as the hero in the fairy-tale *Hansel and Gretel* and drop bread (or peanuts, candies or popcorn) along the way in the hopes that they will mark the trail. Believe it or not, this has actually been (and probably still is) used on many occasions and it never worked any better for those who tried it than it did for the unfortunate Hansel. Birds and small animals will snap up the morsels as fast as you drop them. Chipmunks love popcorn, no peanut is safe for more than ten seconds around a squirrel or a blue jay and smaller animals and insects will also share in the delights you scatter along the way. I sat on a fallen tree one afternoon and watched in amazement as four large, black ants pooled their efforts to cart away a sugar candy I had dropped from my package. It took them twenty minutes of tugging, lugging, pushing, pulling and carrying but they ultimately disappeared with it into the underbrush. No human can hope to outwit insects with such a Calvinist work ethic.

Learn from the mistakes of others and heed the recorded misfortunes of those who have gone before. It offers the advantage of having walked in their shoes, so to speak. Taking a few precautions before heading into the bush will help you avoid getting lost in the first place.

My maternal grandfather, to whose memory this book is dedicated, was a northern Saskatchewan woodsman of unparalleled wisdom in wood lore. During the many years he lived in the Torch River area he helped rescue dozens of people, mostly hunters who had ventured up from Saskatoon or Regina. Invariably, many lost their way. He could never understand why people who knew nothing of the woods would go in so unprepared. He had no patience whatever for those who got lost, holding as he did to the belief that a few precautions were all it took to avoid the situation. Astounding as it may seem, some of those hunters got lost more than once. He had little use for "city folk," as he called them, and none whatever for those stupid enough to get lost more than once.

My grandfather was the leader of a search party which rescued the same hunter on consecutive years. The phrase with which he greeted that unfortunate man is still used in the north woods to sum up duplicity in stupidity: "Not even a cat would jump onto a hot stove," he said to the poor fellow. "And he sure wouldn't be doing it twice."

Grandfather didn't care a great deal for cats but he gave them credit for being infinitely smarter than "city folk" who got lost in the bush.

So be smart and envision the woods in the same way my grandfather's cat regarded stoves. Don't venture into the bush so unprepared that circumstances may make things too hot for you to deal with competently.

3 Preparing a Survival Kit

Whether you plan to fly, drive, canoe, ride horse-back or hike into a wilderness area anywhere in North America, you should never set out without a basic survival kit. Many people who are lost each year, providing they are finally found, admit to having ventured thoughtlessly into the woods with insufficient gear for survival or, equally as bad, having carried useless things. Limit your kit to necessities. An entire case of tinned food is of no use if you have no way to open the tins; and a bottle of medicine is dangerous if you don't know its use. Know what you have, anticipate what you might need before you leave and know how much to take with you.

For basic survival you will ideally carry the following: (These are minimum amounts, extra food never hurts.)

a. Twelve four-foot lengths of sturdy twine or a roll of strong string measuring a minimum of forty-eight feet.
b. Three twelve-foot lengths of quarter-inch hemp (or nylon) rope.
c. At least one wide-blade knife (or similar sturdy knife).
d. A hatchet or small ax, preferably with a carrying holster.
e. About forty-eight feet of copper wire, tightly coiled.
f. One reel of heavy-test fish line, two reels are better.
g. A dozen steel, barbed fish hooks of assorted sizes.
h. One large flashlight with spare batteries and bulbs.
i. A warm blanket (two are better).
j. Three empty (sixteen-ounce or one-liter) cylindrical tins with plastic lids (big coffee tins are **ideal**).
k. Safety matches in a waterproof container.
l. One 500 tablet bottle of aspirin (generic ASA bottles of 500 are available at low cost at discount drugstores). A pack of safety pins. Six 8" x 8" squares of cotton cloth. A bottle of iodine. A package of gauze. Two rolls of **wide** adhesive tape. A flask of

rum. A pair of scissors. A box of baking soda. A couple of pencils and a writing pad.

m. Packets of sugar and salt, instant coffee, juice powder, powdered milk, hot chocolate, tea bags, bouillon cubes and several high-protein candy bars (available in camper supplies stores).

n. A plastic or metal whistle with a loud tone.

o. A reasonable compass. (See below for using your wristwatch as a compass.)

p. This book.

Sounds like an awful lot, doesn't it! The above list looks like a lot but it is not. The food supplies, if carefully rationed, will keep you going about fourteen days.

How to pack for compactness

Experienced backpackers know the idea in bush travel is to keep the pack small and light—no one goes into the woods carrying a suitcase. Those who ride trails know all that is required will fit into a blanket roll which can be tied behind the saddle or kept in a couple of saddle bags. An emergency kit is no different and can be either rolled or shaped into a compact, square bundle.

First lay the blanket(s) on a flat surface. In one of the tins place the packets of sugar, salt, instant hot chocolate, tea, coffee, milk, a bouillon cube (i.e., Oxo) and juice powder. The tin should be full and if it is not, add enough extra packets to fill it. Replace the lid and seal with adhesive tape.

Now roll your ASA, safety pins, one roll of adhesive tape, iodine, flask of rum, gauze, compass and scissors in the cotton cloths. Roll tightly so it will fit into the second tin. Replace top and seal with adhesive tape from the second roll.

In the third tin place your fish line, hooks (all packaged safely in a small envelope), safety matches (tape the heads to prevent accidents and tape the box completely as extra precaution). Put in your extra knife, the spare flashlight batteries and the bulbs. Pack the tin tightly with extra packs of dry goods (coffee, tea and juice powder). Replace lid and seal with adhesive tape. Tape your note pad upright on the outside of the tin along with your pencil(s).

Return to the blanket. Place all but three of your sturdy twine ropes with your hemp or nylon rope—**lengthwise**—at the center of the blanket. Put your three tins—end to end—**across** the ropes one foot from the bottom. Place your hatchet, second roll of adhesive tape, flashlight, knives, box of baking soda, and coil of copper wire above the tins. **Put this book on the top and secure it with a strip of tape.** There is a good reason for this: The book will help you only if it is with you. It will do no good whatsoever if it is at home in a drawer. Don't leave home without it.

Note: If your hatchet is in a carrying holster, leave it out for attachment to your belt as it is better to have it at hand. Hang the whistle around your neck. If you wish, you can carry the compass as well.

Now draw the left and right edges of the blanket inward toward the middle and overlap so everything within is very snug. Starting from the bottom, roll the blanket into as tight a roll as possible. Use the three ropes you set aside to tie the roll tightly in three places. The outside ropes should be no more than three inches from each end; the middle one dead center. (Duct tape is useful in making a secure secondary seal.) The roll will weigh under six pounds and can be easily stowed in a backpack, behind a saddle, in the trunk of the car, in the bow of a canoe or boat or secured elsewhere, including on your back. Because it is light, it will be easy to carry.

If you want a square pack simply rearrange the tins, etc., so the blankets will fold instead of roll. Tie the pack with the three ropes, evenly spaced, to encircle the entire pack. As with the roll, duct tape makes a secure secondary seal.

The breakdown of how this emergency pack will be employed is as follows: the long ropes will be used in the construction of a lean-to plus a variety of uses including the main line of a fishing net. The short ones will be used in your shelter and have many other uses. The copper wire will be used for snares, but can also double as an antenna in case you have access to a radio.

The fish line, besides its intended use, can be woven into a gill-net, be used as a night line, become part of your shelter or be used in whatever way you will be able to think of later, including mending torn clothing. That is why two reels are recommended.

The hatchet will cut your firewood, help build your shelter, blaze trails and have a dozen other uses including that of a defensive weapon.

The notebook will allow you to keep an account of your daily activities, important for morale purposes and as a record of your trials and travails for future reference. Also, it will identify you should rescue, heaven forfend, come too late or if your remains are not found for many years. While not a pleasant thought it is a necessary consideration. Not everyone gets out, after all.

The ASA will help you overcome sprains and minor hurts. The iodine will clean and disinfect cuts and a drop in your daily drinking water will help guard against goiter problems over a long run. If the salt in your food pack is iodized don't use the iodine for other than tending wounds. Use iodine sparingly as it tends to burn the wound which sometimes hinders healing.

The packets of bouillon and the candy bars will supply you with enough nutrition to keep you going while you learn to gather edible plants, snare animals and catch fish.

Baking soda, one of the world's finest multi-use wonder products, will serve almost every purpose from alleviating insect stings to soothing burns and plant rashes. It can be used as tooth powder. A quarter of a teaspoon of soda in a coffee tin of boiling water will tenderize the toughest fibrous edible plant including plantain. It will also ease foot rash and help prevent rash when sprinkled lightly into your socks.

The coffee, tea, juice, milk powder, sugar and salt will make life a little more bearable while you learn the harsh lessons of bush survival.

The three tins, will serve as cooking utensils and berry gathering containers. They will provide whatever service they will be called on to perform—including rain collectors for water supply. The adhesive tape will serve a number of useful purposes including substitutes for strings and ropes.

The referee's whistle will attract the attention of passing rescuers who may not otherwise hear or see you. It can also be used to frighten away undesirable small animals.

Warning! Caution!: Never! Never! Never! use a whistle in an attempt to scare off wolverines. This animal will be not the least impressed as they do not frighten. A bear **might** amble off, depending on its mood of the moment, but a wolverine will become enraged whereupon you will, to your sorrow, witness the definitive description of "savage beast." It is to your advantage simply to remain as invisible as you can (see Chapter 15).

The following chapters will show you how to properly utilize everything in the emergency roll, how to use the forest to your advantage, how to recognize, gather and prepare the more easily recognizable edible plants, how to catch and prepare birds, animals and insects as food (yes, I said insects), and how to recognize those things you **must** avoid. You will be guided, step by step, through the not-all-that-mysterious world of the woods, bush and forests of North America and shown the ways of survival.

Note: If you elect not to pack a compass or should lose yours, utilize your watch as a compass. This is an easy procedure but only works when the sun is visible. Hold the watch flat in your hand. Point the hour hand directly at the sun. The 12 will indicate approximate south. North will be directly opposite at 6. East will be 9 and west will be 3.

If your watch is digital this method obviously won't work. However, it will tell you the time so simply draw a circle on a piece of paper or a slab of bark or anything else that is flat. Place numbers, as properly spaced as possible, around the outside of the circle—clockwise—from 1 to 12. Make sure the 12 is directly opposite the 6 and the 9 is directly opposite the 3. Check the time on your digital watch and mark the closest hour to the corresponding number on your paper. If, for instance it is 2:45 move to 3:00 but if it is 2:15 use 2:00 as the marker. For an accurate reading wait until an exact hour is reached.

Turn your card until the hour number points **directly** at the sun. Like a conventional clock the 12 will indicate due south and 6 gives you north. Compass readers always use north as the focal point, it makes the going easier. It is a good idea to attach some marker to a tree (or make an arrow out of stones or twigs) pointing north for easy future reference.

You can make a permanent compass easily enough. Pierce two, small, light twigs with a needle directly through their middles. It will look like this: ++. Place them in a pool of still water or in a wooden bowl filled with water. Make certain nothing metal is close by. The twigs will float keeping the needle flat on the surface as the needle slowly turns. When it has stopped turning the needle's widest point will be pointing to magnetic north.

If both ends are equal in size, or if you are uncertain for any reason, wait for a sunny day or clear night. At high noon the sun will be due south. Check the needle against the sun. The point **opposite** is your north pointer. On a clear night check the needle against the north star. The end pointing toward the star is the north pointer. Mark the proper end for future reference.

If you have no watch, make a sundial. First determine the north/south line and:

a. Draw a circle on the ground or on a flat rock.

b. Draw numbers or place stones—**clockwise**—from 1 to 12 on both sides of the circle. Use a large stone for **north 12**, this will be the reference point. Be certain the 12s are at due north and due south. East and west will be at the 6s.

c. An upright twig, dead center in the circle, serves as a dial. As the sun moves from east to west the twig will cast its shadow across the number or the rock which indicates the correct time. A.M. will be to the right and P.M. will be to the left side. (Remember, the sun is always on standard time.)

At night, as stated earlier, north is easily found by locating the big dipper (Ursa Major) which points to the north star. Draw an arrow in the dirt or lay an arrow made of stones or twigs as a pointer to North. **It is very important for anyone lost in the woods to know how to determine proper compass points**, especially if the time comes when walking out is considered the best or only viable option.

4 Building a Shelter

Anyone lost in the wilderness is in trouble from the moment he ventures off the beaten path until the minute he is found. It matters little if he is 1,000 miles or 1,000 feet from safety because distance in a forest is often irrelevant. If no one knows where you are, there is no immediate way of them helping you out of your predicament. The best thing for you to do is to realize—and accept—that:

a. You are lost.
b. In all likelihood no one has missed you yet.
c. It will be hours—perhaps days—before a search is begun.
d. You will probably remain lost for at least seven days.
e. You had better think of finding shelter.
f. You have very little daylight left.

First things first, though. Take a few moments to sit down and think things out. If you have any injuries—no matter how minor—tend to them at once. Follow priorities. Tend to breaks, deep cuts and sprains, first; bruises and abrasions, second.

Clean, if necessary bandage, all cuts and scratches; the last thing you need is an infection which might lead to blood poisoning. That done, you can start looking for a site to build a shelter. It will ideally have water, protection against animals, be away from incidental dangers and in a place searchers will be able to spot. Do not worry at this time about finding the **ideal** site. That can wait a day or two. What you need now is a good temporary site on which to build a lean-to.

If you are in heavy bush or forest you should choose the most open place in the immediate area. If you are in a desert, open space is less of a problem; but desert and Arctic survival procedures are not dealt with in-depth in this book as they are extensive subjects unto themselves.

It may not always be possible to find water immediately, but if you are in forested or mountainous country, water will be close at hand. Water in the desert is actually present most of the time. It is always deep beneath the ground but is readily available in the pulp of cacti. (Locating water is dealt with in Chapter 12.)

Incidental dangers encountered in the selection of a site cover a fairly wide range so it is wise to know what they are and how to avoid them. First, **never** camp right on the bank of a stream or river, on what appears to be a dry river bed, in an arroyo or in a dry gulch. If the words "flash flood" hold little meaning for you at the moment, they will in the seconds before a torrent of rushing water sweeps you and your camp away, probably into the hereafter.

The main argument against lake, river and stream banks is the probability of an intolerable abundance of forest insects. Mosquitos in particular hover near water. Though less dangerous than flash floods and bears, mosquitos are capable of causing you more grief than you may be able to handle. In the woods, forests and swampy areas of North America each mosquito swarm numbers in the hundreds of thousands. If you get into a swarm of mosquitos they can very quickly drive you out of your mind. Opt for higher ground.

If you can locate water right away, so much the better. Cattails usually grow in abundance near water and these plants will immediately solve your food problems. Camp close enough to the water that a long trek is unnecessary, but stay far enough away that the above-mentioned dangers are minimized. If there is a rise or a short hill nearby, use it; it will be easier for rescuers to see you from the air.

If there is no immediate water available, do not fret over it as that wastes time and on your first day time is important. Concentrate on erecting a lean-to. Then you can utilize what remains of daylight to look around. Tomorrow is soon enough to spend in the search for water; and you can always move if you find a better site.

It is also wise to remember that animals such as bears, cougars and wolves visit lakes, water holes, streams and rivers to drink. Therefore do not camp on or beside a trail animals use to reach their watering spot or you may regret it, particularly if a bear wants a drink and decides that you are in his way. Remember this: bears are sociopaths not given to sharing with others. (See the drawings of animal spoor at the back of the book for easy identification of the animals that use the trail.)

Once you have determined your site, you must quickly begin construction of a shelter. All you need is two stout trees for uprights and seven or eight sturdy poles—one for a cross bar, three for slope-poles and three as cross poles. Do not try to get by with less than three slope-poles (four are best) in order to give maximum support to your roof. You will require a great many boughs (fir or spruce are best), some string or rope and something with which to trim the poles. Now you know why an ax or hatchet and string or rope are such important parts of a survival kit. If you have no ax or hatchet you will have to rip the needed material from the trees. Not neat, certainly, but effective enough. (See Chapter 16 if you have absolutely no survival gear.)

Step One: you must find two stout trees of reasonable girth (a **minimum** of three inches in diameter, which means about a 10" circumference and at least ten feet tall) standing three to five feet apart. Trim the lower branches to a height of five feet. Clear the surrounding area of rocks, fallen branches, etc.

Step Two: locate a crossbar. This can be a fallen sapling but make sure it is sturdy. The crossbar should extend at least one foot beyond each of the uprights (see diagram #1). Tie the crossbar to the uprights at a height of two to five feet. (In building a lean-to take a tip from the animals: animals choose a den with a low entrance because it is not easily seen and has a certain degree of difficulty for entry. Besides, the lower it is, the easier it will be to construct. With that in mind keep your lean-to low, but remember to allow for room to sit upright.)

If you do not have string or rope, use narrow strips of birch or any other bark which will rip away easily. Long stalks of coarse grass or cattail leaves woven together also do a good job. Gather many stalks of grass or cattails and tie them, three or four stalks at a time, together into strands. More than four stalks can be too stiff to loop into the required knots and less may lack needed strength. Wrap the strands around each tree and the crossbar's ends in a figure eight as tightly as possible (see diagram #1). Tuck in the ends. You may need two or three such strands to make a secure tie.

Step Three: locate three or four sturdy slope-poles (1" diameter in seven- to ten-foot lengths). The longer the slope-poles the deeper your lean-to will be. These may be saplings already fallen or ones you cut yourself. Sharpen one end of each if possible. Force the sharp ends into the ground so the poles rest against the crossbar at an angle of 30° to 45°. Place the poles at even intervals along the crossbar and tie them securely. Instead of using twine or rope you can notch both the crossbar and slope-poles so you can fit them snugly together. You now have completed a frame. (See diagram #1.)

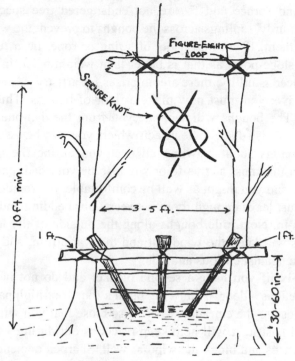

Building a shelter, the basic frame.

Step Four: collection of boughs can now begin. Select long, heavily needled boughs of fresh spruce or fir. Avoid pine boughs. Pine needles are much too long, too sparse and very sharply pointed. Lay the boughs along the slope poles, needles pointing downwards with the branch wood on the underside. Employ the same principal as laying a roof on a house: start at the bottom, work upward toward the crossbar, overlapping each bough by at least a foot but by no more than half the length of the one under it. When you finish take a good look at your "roof" from inside the lean-to. You will see immediately if there are sparse spots as the light will shine through. These areas should be reinforced.

Depending on the thickness of the boughs you select, your "roof" will be within a scale of very poor to very good. **Never** settle for anything less than very good. The last thing you want is leaks in case of rain or to have your roof blown off during a heavy wind. Put on as many layers of boughs as needed. Don't scrimp; Mother Nature is generous and spruce and fir are not endangered tree species. Lay fallen, but sturdy, saplings across the boughs to prevent the wind from disrupting them. If you have lots of string or rope, tie a few loops across the slope-poles as that is better than weighting it. In survival what you need is utility; there are no prizes for artistry.

Step Five: you must now make a floor of boughs. This is very necessary. The boughs will separate you from the dampness of the ground. It will also discourage insects which, you may be assured, will have no qualms about crawling all over you during the night. Be generous in thickness as this floor will also be your bed, perhaps for many days, and you might as well be comfortable; but remember also that you must leave enough room between your bedding and the roof of the lean-to. Next, pile boughs along the outside of the lean-to as walls. This will keep the wind out and the warmth in, and serve as camouflage against curious animals.

Step Six: if you have a second blanket and do not need it for warmth use it as a door. Otherwise, build a four-foot-high palisade of saplings close to the entrance. Make it so close that you will have to sidle to get past it. It will help keep raccoons out during your occasional absences and block the wind as well. Sharpen one end of each sapling and drive it into the ground as deeply as you can. Place them close together, preferably touching. The finished effort will look like the wall of a wooden fort. It is a wise added touch, but is mainly an option used for permanent sites.

Note: It is much better to build a lean-to than to seek shelter in a cave. What you may think is the perfect cave may well be an animal's dream home and it will certainly object to your presence. Caves also house bats and they are often rabid. Avoid caves.

If you change your camp, leave a note in the abandoned lean-to with information such as the circumstances of its existence, your identity, the date and the direction you are heading. Such data will prove helpful to any searchers who come upon it.

With your temporary home finished you should now light a fire. Your fireplace **must** be built on cleared ground, in a shallow pit enclosed within a circle of stones which will help keep the fire from spreading. The fire should be reasonably close to the lean-to. It is advisable to keep a small fire going all night to provide some warmth and keep animals from venturing too closely. (Fire and its care is covered in Chapter 16.)

That is all that is required for a sturdy, comfortable, temporary shelter. It takes less than three hours to build a well-constructed lean-to and start a proper fire. These should be the third and fourth items on your agenda after treatment of injuries and choosing the location for your campsite.

Obviously this is something that must be done before daylight is gone. Otherwise, you will be out all night in a coal black, usually cold, always frightening, alien and often-dangerous environment. If darkness is fast approaching move the shelter construction to a higher priority and don't worry so much about location.

Be alert to the need for maintenance. If you are not rescued readily and have to stay longer than a few days, the floor of your lean-to will have to be changed as the boughs dry out. Roofs generally last longer but you must be careful to avoid dryness to a point where fire becomes a hazard. The last thing you need is to be caught in a forest fire, especially one you have caused yourself.

For latrine purposes, remember you are alone so you can forget about modesty. Go a good fifty feet away from your campsite and scrape a shallow hole in the ground, use it, then cover it with dirt, loose gravel or whatever is handy so flies and other nuisance insects will not be attracted. If you think you would feel better with a more permanent latrine it must be dug fairly deeply at least fifty feet from your lean-to and away from the water source and it will also need a cover. This can wait until you decide whether or not to move to a better, more-permanent site.

A latrine is not recommended for urination. Urinate against trees 100 to 150 feet from your site. Use a different tree each time until you eventually "ring" your campsite. This little ritual will "mark" your territory in the same manner employed by most wild animals. It is a sort of "language" animals understand and, because the scent will likely be unfamiliar to them, they will be more apt to keep their distance rather than risk a challenge from an unknown and potential enemy.

Summing up

You need a lean-to no later than one hour after sunset the first night. A fire is also a main consideration. Other concerns can wait until morning. Use the remainder of the evening to tend to whatever minor wounds you might have. Plantain, which grows nearly everywhere, makes an exceptionally good bandage for cuts and scratches, as the plant contains a congealing agent which will hasten healing. Pick fresh, broad, green leaves and "bruise" them by rubbing your fingers and thumbs down them. Or you can crinkle them if you wish—anything to break the surface. Bruising is best.Lay the leaves across the wounds and cuts. Secure them firmly in place. Replace with new leaves every two hours (see Chapter 7).

5 Identifying Edible Plants

There are hundreds of varieties of edible plants in the wilds of North America but the purpose of this book is to introduce the lost traveler only to those considered best for emergency use in survival. Most grow plentifully throughout the continent and all can be used in emergency situations. The plants and trees listed below are found in most parts of North America although some are limited to specific areas. Regional plants are identified as such. Certain parts of some plants are toxic and these are noted with a specially marked warning which points out the toxic parts.

There are several species of shrubs and trees that can be used for emergency foods through their inner bark and certain seeds. These are listed. In some trees, sap can be used as a quick energy food or as a sometimes palatable chewing gum. The root and bark of the white willow is an excellent source of ASA. If you are lost along the coast of B.C., Washington or Oregon or from Labrador to points south along the eastern seaboard, do not turn your nose up at seaweed and other forms of kelp. You enjoyed kelp within the past month and probably never knew it. The mayonnaise on your last sandwich and the ice cream you had for dessert likely contained agar which is made from marine algae and other forms of kelp.

If a person is so hopelessly lost that rescue will be a matter of a long time, he or she is advised to make ready for a lengthy stay in the bush—not everyone is fortunate enough to be rescued quickly. This means that survival may well depend on storing foods for future use, drying certain roots for flour and starch and drying seeds and leaves for use in teas and soups.

Survival is an extremely serious business and hard work is always a part of being found alive and well. Indeed, hard work usually spells the difference between living and dying. Survival may well depend on how quickly—and how well—you learn to identify the plants which will keep you alive and how to avoid those which will kill you.

When cooking leaves and tender stalks, use very little water. Even when conservation of water is not important, use as little as possible. Remember also that minimal water will come to a boil quicker, thereby conserving your fire wood. Remember the word **allocate** in the anagram. Often the water within the plant is sufficient, as leaves and tender stalks require little time to cook (usually 3 to 10 minutes). Because boiling always removes precious vitamins and minerals from the food, keep the water in which the plant was boiled and, when it is cool, drink it.

Leaves and tender shoots can also be steamed if you have a steam-pit readied. Roots and older stalks, which tend to be woody, require a longer time to soften. They should be boiled with extra water to ensure the water does not boil away. Also, a pinch of your baking soda in the water will hasten the softening process.

Following is the list of the plants which will help you survive.

Acorns (*Quercus*)

These nuts from the oak tree kept peasants in the dark ages from starving during days of famine and siege. In some cases they were the only food available for entire villages. Acorns are easily identified as they look something like hazelnuts with a greenish gray hat on top. Eat them roasted, boiled or raw, but first you must leach them to remove the tannin, a bitter substance which isn't harmful. Leaching takes little effort and requires a few days. You must allow running water to wash over the nuts. This can be accomplished by breaking open the nuts, placing the harvest in a corral of rocks in a shallow section of a stream where the flowing water will wash over them without carrying them away. Leave them there for two to five days, depending on the number involved, and the leaching will be adequate. A net bag or a large tin with holes in it would be ideal for the leaching process.

Balsam fir (*Abies balsamea*)

A tall evergreen tree which grows to a great height in the shape of a church steeple. Needles are about an inch in length and have two white lines on the underside. Cones grow to three inches (7.5 cm) in length and are purple to green. The cones grow in erect position to the bough and the seeds are **inside** the cones. Balsam trees are found in cool woods throughout Canada and in the U.S. as far south as Virginia.

Balsam sap boiled to a thin syrup makes a good throat soother if used three times a day, a teaspoon at a time. It tastes terrible but it works, sort of a cough medicine with an attitude. When the pitch is boiled, its steam is a great aid to breathing in case of sinus congestion. The inner bark can be dried and then powdered to make a palatable flour to thicken gruels and stews. It has many vitamins.

Bear berries (*Arctostaphylos uva-ursi*) also known as kinnikinik and bear's grape

The botanical names translate as "bear's grape, bear's grape." That seems a little redundant, somehow, so we shall call them bear berries. This plant is found from the high Arctic into the northern United States. It grows low as a trailing shrub and prefers being under exposed rock and in sandy places. The plant has reddish, paperlike bark, with leaves that are small and shaped like paddles. It has pink or white egg-shaped flowers with fluted openings. Berries are red and, because they can be eaten raw, make a great emergency fruit. Leaves, when dried, can be used as a reasonable substitute for a nicotine-free tobacco for those hooked on smoking. One would think that being lost in the woods would be the ideal time to kick the smoking habit.

Black crowberries (*Empetrum nigrum*)

A low shrub, matlike in appearance, it has tiny, pink flowers which hide between pairs of flat, needlelike leaves. The fruit is a juicy, black berry about the size of a garden pea. It grows from the Arctic into the northern U.S. They can be eaten direct from the bush. Black crowberries are far more flavorful **after** freezing so they make an excellent winter emergency food. Crowberries grow in great abundance on the tundra. They are also prolific in peat soil. Remember also that peat, when dried, makes excellent slow-burning fuel for your fire.

Buffaloberry (*Shepherdia argentea*)

An excellent survival food found throughout Canada and northern U.S., the plant grows to ten feet. The leaves are elliptic to oval, dark green on top and rusty silver underside. The raw fruit, a red berry, has a disagreeable taste. Therefore, boil the berries and allow the water to cool for a fine tea filled with nutrients. The boiled berries can be eaten but are recommended only as a last resort as they are not good tasting.

In the west the silver buffaloberry prevails. It closely resembles the ordinary buffaloberry, but the plant is slightly thorny with silver leaves and the fruit is a very dark red. Both are cooked the same way.

Bulrushes (*Scirpus acutus*)

A truly versatile emergency food, found throughout North America in wetlands and swamps, and along creeks, lakes, sloughs and rivers. Bulrushes, which resemble cattails, grow in dense stands. They are tall and dark green. The stems are smooth and round, without leaves, and topped by branches of brown, bristled flower spikes which cluster. The root is thick and scaly. Use the roots, shoots, seeds and pollen.

Young shoots are eaten either raw or boiled; old shoots should be pared to the tender cores which are then used in the same fashion as young shoots. The rootstalks are boiled until soft and eaten as potatoes.

The pollen, which collects as dust on the outside of the shoots, can be shaken off into a dry container and saved as a thickener for soups and stews. Dry the seeds then crush them into flour. Dried roots also can be crushed into flour.

Burdock (*Arctium minus*)

A member of the thistle family, but the leaves are not prickly and will not sting although the rough hairs may cause a minor rash on very sensitive skin. Flowers are purple-red burrs which grow at the top of the plant in the manner of thistles. Found throughout North America in waste ground and dry, open spaces, the entire plant, except the burrs, is edible. Young leaves can be eaten raw but old leaves must be boiled in several changes of water for at least thirty minutes.

Pare the thick covering from roots and boil for thirty minutes. Boil the white pith from the center of the leaf stalks as you would the root. Burdock makes an excellent survival food as it is full of vitamins, particularly vitamin C.

Cattail (*Typha latifolia*)

This is the broad-leaf cattail and is the world's greatest survival food due to its versatility and great abundance. A secondary, lesser cattail (*Typha augustofolia*) differs from *latifolia* only in that it has narrow leaves. *Augustofolia* is equally as excellent as the broad-leaf variety and the difference is mentioned only because some people have refused to use the narrow-leaf cattail because they didn't know what it was. The lost traveler can survive for months on cattails alone, years if necessary.

Found in every area of North America in swamps, along the shores of lakes, rivers, creeks, ponds, wet meadows and sloughs. They can be eaten raw or cooked. You will know where to find cattails when you see red-winged blackbirds. These birds use the wool from old cattails to build their nests.

Pare the tender, young shoots to their white core. Eat raw or boil like asparagus. Young stalks are prepared in like manner. The immature flower spikes should be boiled a few minutes. Large amounts of pollen can easily be gathered by shaking the heads into a dry container. Use the same as starch or flour after drying.

In winter short sprouts begin to grow from the underwater roots. These sprouts can be boiled. In winter pare the roots and stalks to the white core and boil for a protein-filled, but rather starchy, survival food.

Chickweed (*Stellaria media*)

Very common everywhere (you have likely cursed this plant as you hauled it out of your lawn and garden), this plant is a truly useful emergency plant for food and medicine. Tender, juicy, pale-green stems will reach a foot in length. Chickweed is one of the hardiest plants around, yet it is so weak that it never raises off the ground more than an inch or so. Green leaves grow opposite each other every quarter-inch or so along stems. Each leaf is half-an-inch long and one-quarter-inch across, egg-shaped and ending in a small point.

Flowers are small, white and star-shaped with five petals. The petals are deeply cleft at outer ends and grow about a quarter inch across. Flowers open midmorning on sunny days, but on cloudy or rainy days stay closed. At night, plants and leaves close up together as if cuddled in sleep.

Eat leaves raw or cooked with the stems. Makes a great two-course meal. Simmer a goodly amount of chickweed in eight ounces of hot water. Let it infuse for twenty minutes. Remove the chickweed and eat, then drink the tea.

Note: Chickweed is medicinally useful as a poultice in treating boils, sores and external ulcers (see Chapter 7).

Chufa (*Cyperus esculentis*) also known as nut-grass

Although limited in its uses, chufa is a great emergency food and is plentiful in wet or damp areas. It is found everywhere from the east coast to the Pacific coast in Canada and the U.S. Along the Pacific coast it grows abundantly from Alaska well into Mexico. A relation to the bulrush, it has grassy leaves at the base and a stout triangular seed-stalk of one to two feet in height. Near the top of the stalk is a second circle of leaves, similar to the base leaves but smaller. Above the stem leaves is a flower cluster of five to eight rays each. Each bears numerous flat spikelets.

The only useful part of the chufa is the bulb. Pull the roots gently in order to get as many as possible. Because these bulbs are only a half-inch in length, many are needed. Do not worry about depleting this plant as the bulbs you miss from each plant will more than replenish those you use. They are not very tasty when raw but when roasted or baked they are as good as peanuts and they are full of nutrients.

If you harvest a large number, roast at the edge of the fire until very brown and dry, but not burned. Crush and grind them, between two flat rocks, into as fine a powder as possible and use as coffee. The resulting drink is very near to being as tasty as any commercial coffee but has no caffeine. Chufas are excellent medicine for an upset digestive system (see Chapter 7).

Clover (many species) (*Trifolium spp.*)

A shamrocklike plant, it is easily identified by its three leaflets and dense pea-like white to pinkish flowers. It is a versatile food because the leaves, flowers and seeds can be used as tea, boiled greens or flour. Mix clover flowers with Labrador tea or Jersey tea for improved flavor. It is rich in protein.

Boil leaves for not less than twenty minutes. Use sparingly as the tea acts as a laxative in some people. You will soon learn your personal limits. Found everywhere in North America. It is probably a myth that four-leafed clovers bring good luck but when you are lost it doesn't hurt to look for one or two along the way. After all, you need all the help available.

Cow parsnip (*Hercaleum lanatum*) also known as masterwort

Very large, wooly, rank stalks which are hollow and ridged. Flower clusters grow to eight inches across and smell as musty as a long-closed room. Leaves grow more than twelve inches in length in a three-pronged maple leaf shape. The leaf stalks have swollen bases. Use only mature plants as young plants can be confused with hemlock. Found in moist ground and thickets throughout Canada and in the northern states from the western mountains as far east as Georgia.

Young stems and leafstalks **must** be peeled. Boiled for fifteen minutes they taste like celery. Change water at least three times to remove strong flavor. Tender roots, which are boiled like parsnips, were a mainstay in the diets of many Native tribes, but the taste does not really appeal to modern palates. Seeds, when dried, make good seasoning.

Warning: Do not mistake hemlock for cow parsnip. The stalks are the clue. (See hemlock to compare differences.)

Dandelion (*Taraxacum officinale*)

Everyone knows what a dandelion looks like and anyone can eat it without ill effects. It grows everywhere and is always plentiful. It is an exceptional emergency food because leaves, flowers, stems and roots all have their uses. Young, tender leaves and stems should be quick-boiled or steamed. Flower petals can be eaten raw. Dry the roots thoroughly, then crush and boil for a pretty good coffeelike beverage filled with vitamins. You will need many roots as the drink tastes better when it is brewed stronger.

Field garlic (*Allium verneale*)

A tall, singular stalk with numerous pink flowers at top, it has the odor of onions. The bulbs can be eaten raw or used in stews. The leaves can be eaten. It is found mainly in the northern U.S., but has been found in southern Canada over the last few years.

Its cousin wild garlic (*Allium canadense*) is found from northern Canada south to Texas. Wild garlic causes a lingering odor when eaten, whereas field garlic does not. It is doubtful that a survivor would care all that much about a lingering odor. After all, who is around to be offended?

Juneberry (*Amelanchier alnifolia*) also known as serviceberry, Saskatoon berry and shadberry

Grows as shrubs or small trees. The leaves are oval with sharp tips and slightly toothed along the edges. Flowers, white with five petals, grow in clusters that droop. The berries, purple to black are sweet and juicy. Several species have bitter berries but a single berry will determine the trait so the remainder can be avoided. An excellent survival food, they grow in abundance on river banks and lake shores. They can be eaten uncooked straight from the bush. If you have a surplus supply, simmer the berries which you can then eat while drinking the tea. They are filled with vitamin C.

Kelp (*Macrocystis*)

Kelp, or seaweed as it is more commonly known, is found in abundance from north to south along both west and east coasts. Easily identifiable, kelp floats in large colonies. Some species have tendrils that look like ropes and extend to 200 feet. These colonies are kept afloat by large bulbs. (Each bulb, for which there is no use to the survivor, contains enough carbon monoxide to kill a full-grown chicken within sixty seconds.)

To use kelp as an emergency food, choose the smallest plants as these will be more tender. Cut into short strips, boil in fresh water for ten minutes or so then leave it to infuse. It will produce a rich, brown liquid that is aromatic and flavorful. Use this liquid to cook fish or small animals. Add some water-lily tubers and some sliced cattail cores. The result is a tasty stew.

Use as a broth to turn a squirrel or rabbit or a filleted carp into a hearty soup. If you are cooking meat, take a cup of the liquid, bring to the boil, thicken with cattail or bulrush pollen and enjoy meat and gravy. Kelp is loaded with vitamins, iodine and potassium, all of which are good for you.

Labrador tea (*Ledum groenlandicum*)

Each specie resembles the other. Another of the finest emergency foods in North America, it is found everywhere in Canada from Newfoundland to Vancouver Island and throughout the northern U.S. This low, evergreen bush produces small, dull-gray, leathery, untoothed leaves with slightly rolled-up edges and white (sometimes rusty) wool on the underside. They resemble little canoes. The leaves remain on the plant year-round which makes it the perfect source of survival food.

Steep leaves in boiled water for ten minutes. The tea is mild and has enough vitamin C in one six-ounce serving to supply an average person all day.

Drink Labrador tea during the first few days almost exclusively as its nutrients will keep you going long enough to search out and gather other, more filling plants. If you remembered to pack some salt in your survival kit add a pinch to the tea and, with a bit of imagination, it will actually taste like chicken soup. Limit your intake for the first two days to about eight ounces a day as Labrador tea in large amounts tends to affect some people in a laxatory way.

May-apple (*Podophyllum peltatum*) also known as mandrake

Flowers grow singly. They are white, waxy and have six to nine petals. Fruit, when mature, is a large, yellow, oval berry. Plants grow twelve to eighteen inches (30—45 cm) tall. One umbrella-like leaf will shade the one single berry which comes of the single flower described above. Use only the mature berries.

Warning: Never use the leaves, seeds, root or stalk for any purpose as they are highly cathartic. The root, which vaguely resembles a walking human form, contains a resin which, when extracted and mixed with water, produces *podophyllin*, a pain-killer. When used with extreme care—and in very small doses—this is a good medicine. The mandrake root was so greatly prized by medieval doctors they guarded its medicinal secrets closely by starting all kinds of dark legends about it. Because the average person did not understand the reasons behind the stories, mandrake developed a very bad reputation. It is **not** recommended that survivors use this plant for medicine unless they know the plant and its uses.

Milkweed (*Asclepias speciosa*)

Found throughout North America. Identified by stout, green stalks which exude milky sap when cut into or snapped off. Flowers are domed clusters within the leaf shield. Flowers range from purple-pink to white. Seedpods point upright and are grayish and warty. Plants grow to a height of five feet (1.5 m).

Milkweed is another versatile plant as all of it can be used. Leaves, young shoots and small stems must be boiled for at least fifteen minutes for **each** of three changes of boiling water, four changes is better. Flowers, young pods and top leaves should also be boiled. A clue to finding milkweed is the presence of red-winged blackbirds who use the wool for nesting material when they can't find cattails.

Warning: Do not mistake dogbane or butterfly-weed for milkweed. Dogbane shoots are very hairy and butterfly-weed has a very watery sap. Milkweed has thick, milky sap and its shoots are downy.

Mints

There are so many types of mints that there is no use listing all their generic names. Suffice it to say, all mints belong to the *Mentha* group. They are easily identifiable by individual taste and aroma. Spearmint and peppermint are the best as they make aromatic, vitamin-filled teas and can be used to flavor meats. If you should catch a snake, bake the meat with a handful of mint leaves. Delicious!!

Mint plants, all of which grow throughout North America, are aromatic, have squarish stems, twinned leaves (a leaf on either side of the stalk often shading one or more berries) and small, bluish flowers which cluster near the leaves and stems or at the top as elongated spikes. Use the leaves, fresh or dried, to make tea by simmering for five minutes if dried or ten minutes if fresh. Most mints contain vitamin C, all settle the digestive system and many offer a certain soothing relief to a lost person.

Catnip (*Nepeta cataria*)

Falls vaguely into the mint family although the flowers (bluish with violet spots) cluster only at the very top of the stalk and their odor is unpleasant. Catnip tea, however, becomes pleasantly aromatic and is unquestionably the most soothing of all the teas that can be brewed from wild plants. Catnip does not affect humans as it does cats so you can use it without the fear of running amok, climbing trees, chasing birds or prowling around all night. Quite the opposite will happen as catnip is very soothing. Pour boiling water over the leaves and let infuse for ten minutes.

New Jersey tea (*Ceanothus americanus*)

A low shrub which is woody at the base. Each of its flowers, which grow in oval clusters among the upper leaves, is tiny, white and has five petals. Found in most areas, the leaves, dried, make a fine tea filled with vitamin C. Brew in the same manner as Labrador tea. Mix with clover flowers whenever possible for improved taste. A great number of George Washington's soldiers survived on this tea during the dreadful winter of 1777 during the Revolutionary War.

Orpine (*Sedum telephioides*)

Found from northern Canada to Maryland in open spaces and on hilly banks. This single-stalk plant grows to a thirty-inch (0.75 m) height. It has light green, coarsely-toothed leaves as alternate singles or in groups of three. Flowers of five petals cluster at the top of the plant and are pink to red. The stems are sturdy and fleshy.

The root is made up of many fingerlike tubers. Orpine is extremely versatile. The leaves should be boiled for five to ten minutes and the tubers for twenty minutes. A very good survival food rich in starch, protein and vitamin C.

Oyster plant (*Tragopogon porrifolius*) also known as salsify and purple goat's beard

This plant is similar to one called yellow goat's beard (*Tragopogon pratensis*) and both are edible. Salsify differs from yellow beard only in the purple "rays" which grow from the petals of the salsify's flowers. Yellow grows one to three feet (0.3–1 m) in height while salsify grows two to five feet (0.75–1.5 m).

The flowers (goat's beard's are yellow; salsify's are pink-red to purple) show from dawn until midday when they close up. Both plants are found in most of Canada and in the U.S. from Ohio to Kansas and east to New Jersey. Roots can be boiled as a food or dried and crushed as a coffee substitute. Tender base leaves can be eaten raw but are better when boiled.

Pigweed (*Chenopodium album*) also known as lamb's quarter

Another excellent survival plant. Pigweed grows profusely throughout all of North America and Mexico. This tall weed has many branches. The leaves are fleshy with toothy leaves at the bottom of the plant and narrow, toothless leaves near the top. If you are not sure the plant is pigweed, toss some water on it. If most of the water runs right off, while the remaining water stands in droplets, you will know it is pigweed. The wax in the leaves of the pigweed causes the water to bead. Flowers are small and very, very thickly clustered. They grow in the shelter of the leaves near the stalk. Flowers are greenish with red tinges and produce tiny, black seeds. The plant will grow to three feet (1 m).

Use the tender leaves and plant tips by boiling for ten to fifteen minutes. Boil a large amount as it reduces in volume when cooked, similar to spinach. The seeds are useful too. Boiled, they make a highly nutritious, but rather thin porridge (much like gruel) high in vitamin content. It is particularly good as a breakfast on cold mornings. Its only drawbacks are its color—dark—and a taste which has been described as "mousey." Overcome your squeamishness as this gruel will keep you vigorous and robust all day.

Pine trees (*Pinus spp.*)

As a survival food source the pine tree ranks high. It produces tender needles, an edible inner bark and supplies cones in abundance. Very small cones should be boiled and eaten; large cones produce edible seeds. The inner bark can be powdered into flour. Fresh needles, broken, make an excellent tea rich in vitamins A and C when steeped fifteen to twenty minutes in boiled water. Use the newest needles for the best taste.

Mature cones supply seeds which provide a palatable quick snack when the outer skins are removed. Each cone supplies about fifty seeds. A single tree will supply hundreds of cones depending on its height. **Note: Anyone allergic to nuts must avoid pine seeds**.

Plantain (*Plantago major*)

A top-flight emergency plant. This broad-leaf plant is considered a weed by gardeners. It grows profusely all over North America in open spaces, fields, waste lands and in your lawn if you let it. It is easy to identify by its broad leaves that spread in all directions. The leaves are parallel grained. In the center grows one tall spike of greenish flowers that resembles a oversized pipe cleaner. (Sometimes a plant will grow two or three such spikes.) Young leaves are eaten raw (as a salad). The plant is full of vitamin C and also contains vitamin A. Use the broadest leaves as bandages. They are mildly astringent and will help in the healing of open cuts and wounds. Dried leaves, young or old, make a not-too-bad-tasting medicinal tea. (See Chapter 7.)

Reindeer moss (*Cladonia rangiferina*)

Found from the Arctic (profuse growth) to northern U.S. (sparse growth) on open ground or in partial shade. This moss is a lichen which grows in irregular colonies covering large areas. It has a stalky stem with branches that grow directly out of the stem. Both stem and branches are round and hollow. In wet season the plant is pliable; when dry it is brittle. Use only plants that are silver-gray or ashy. **Never** use yellow or green-gray plants.

Boiling the entire plant will produce a thick soup. If you are fated to a long stay, this plant dries well for future use. Besides soup, reindeer moss also produces flour.

A similar lichen, icelandic moss, grows even farther north and near mountain tops far to the south. It grows as a mat, is brown to olive in color and curls up when dry. Use in same manner as reindeer moss. **Warning**: All lichens are purgative. Soak in cold water for six hours before using. Change the water several times.

Rock tripe (*Umbilicaria mammulata*)

Another edible lichen that grows like a carpet on rocks. Green-gray to khaki-brown it takes an irregular, somewhat circular, shape of one to eight inches across. Like leather when wet, it becomes very brittle when dry. This plant attaches itself to its rock at its center; it can be found on rocks in open woods whether dry or wet. Located throughout the Arctic it extends as far south as Georgia where it does well near mountain tops. Use as a boiled vegetable. Boil gently for an hour or so and add it to your soup or stew. It does not make a soup on its own as does the reindeer moss. **Warning**: This lichen contains an acid which eats into rocks to give a holding grip. This acid produces a **severe** purgative effect in humans unless a few precautions are taken. Any lichen must be soaked at least six hours in cold water with the water being changed several times; but rock tripe must be soaked **no less than eight hours**. Proper soaking neutralizes the acid completely.

Rose hips (*Rosa woodsii*)

If you find yourself among a field of wild roses, rejoice because you won't have to look any further for a means to keeping fit and healthy. Rose hips—the bulb from which the rose petals extend—are filled with vitamin C and E, and the bulb is so pulpy your food problems can be considered over. Rose hips are ready for harvest anytime after August and the old, wrinkled ones from last year are equally good until then, making rose hips an all-year food source. You can eat the fresh hips raw, but always cook the old ones. Either bulb makes very good tea.

To produce a tasty syrup, boil a great amount of old hips and let the water reduce until thick. The syrup keeps well for some time. Pour it over your boiled cattails, thistles or any other vegetable for added taste. Rose hips are so good as an emergency food that when a large group of Canadian explorers went missing in the north woods some fifty years ago they all survived more than a month on nothing but those versatile fruits.

Note: Rose hips contain tiny hairs that can tickle the throat and be annoying. These are easily avoided in your tea and syrup by pouring the liquid through a fine cloth, such as a handkerchief. The hairs do not bother most people.

Skunk cabbage (*Symplocarpus feotidus*)

This plant is included more to warn you off than as a guide to its use. Skunk cabbage is good only as a last resort medicinal plant and should be avoided as food unless absolutely **nothing** else is available. It is included only because it has actually saved a few lives over the years. But as a food—not recommended.

First of all, it smells terrible and that is generally enough to put off anyone no matter how intense the hunger might be. The plant is shell-like with large, mottled yellow or brown leaves which envelop a large, round, fleshy stalk clustered with tiny flowers. First appearance, in early spring, of the cone shows a narrow growth, but as the plant matures the cone spreads outward. The plant will grow to a height of one to three feet (35 cm—1 m). Large green leaves appear after the plant opens and flowers. These leaves are long, wide and pointed. The plant ribs are vertical.

Skunk cabbage is found throughout Canada and northern areas of the U.S. in wet woods and swamp country. The plant can be eaten if the young leaves, **after thorough drying**, are boiled in soups or stews. The roots, **when dried thoroughly**, can be crushed into a coarse flour. Dry by roasting over an open fire. For medicinal purposes see Chapter 7.

Warning: The leaves must **never** be eaten either uncooked or cooked before thorough drying because chemicals within the plant produce an intense burning sensation in the mouth and throat. Also, do not mistake skunk cabbage for false hellebore. (For further information on false hellebore see Chapter 9—Identifying Poisonous Plants.)

Spruce trees (*Picea spp.*)

These trees are easily identified as they are the traditional Christmas tree. They have short, stiff, pointed needles which grow on rough twigs, which in turn grow from thick branches. Unlike fir trees, spruce branches point downwards. The cones droop, are woody and brown. Found throughout North America the various spruces have many uses as a survival food.

Tender shoots can be stripped of their needles and boiled. The inner bark of the tree can be dried and crushed into flour for use in soups or stews. The taste is not very good but the nutritional value overrides that little disadvantage. The pitch, which can be easily removed from the tree's crevices, can be chewed. Saliva is induced which, when swallowed, alleviates minor aches and pains because of the natural ASA the chewing extracts from the pitch.

Spruce needles or pulverized bark can be simmered in water until the liquid is thick. Strain and use as an effective syrup for coughs. It tastes so terrible that it is not likely ever to be overused and that is a good thing as overuse may cause bloating and flatulence. Its taste may well be the original source of the old belief that if medicine doesn't taste good it isn't working. This, however, really works.

Thistles (*Cirsium vulgara*) and nettles (*Urtica dioica*)

All thistles, nettles and burdocks are edible and are found anywhere and everywhere. Most thistles and nettles (except burdock) have prickly leaves and stinging qualities so never gather the leaves unless hands are protected. If you have some sort of digging utensil (a pointed stick will do) dig around the plant until you can firmly grasp the main root (this does not sting) and pull out the entire plant. Remove the burr and other flowers, then boil the complete plant. All prickly qualities are rendered harmless by boiling.

Warning: The prickles and stingers of thistles and nettles can cause a fearsome rash. Handle with great care. If stung, reduce the pain with thick mud or, if you have a survival kit as outlined in a previous chapter, coat the affected area with baking soda then apply a coat of mud. If jewelweed is available, use it as well (see Chapter 8).

Water lilies (many varieties, all edible) (*Nymphaea odorata* is the most common)

Easily recognizable by their large, greenish, flat, dishlike leaves which float in colonies on the surface of lakes and ponds close to shore. Large, showy blossoms, usually pinkish to white, are generally in the center of the pod. Among the most versatile plants in North America, water lilies rank as one of a survivor's truest friends.

Boil the young leaves and unopened flowers for ten minutes. The seeds are rich in protein and can either be boiled or dried and ground into flour. The roots produce brown tubers the size of chicken eggs. Cook the tubers as you would potatoes.

The best way to gather the tubers is to free them from the mud by scuffling along with your bare feet through the colony. The freed roots will float to the surface where you can then remove the largest tubers easily. The roots and the tubers not gathered will sink to grow more lilies. Lilies are found throughout North America near the shores of lakes, along the edges of slow streams and rivers, and all around sloughs, wetlands and swamps.

One feature of water lilies worth remembering is that they invariably mean the presence of frogs. While it is okay to use a small frog or two as bait for a fishing line, please leave the mature bull frogs alone.

Note: It is advisable that frogs not be used for food. First, many species of frogs are becoming endangered and one bull frog will fertilize thousands of eggs from a number of females, monogamy not being in their nature. The loss of one bull means irreplaceable loss to the ecosystem. Secondly, only the legs are edible so there are many more better food sources at hand. The loss of a few small frogs for bait, on the other hand, is not viewed with alarm.

Water parsnip (*Sium suave*)

Warning! Warning!
1. Water parsnip resembles water hemlock but parsnip stems are strongly ridged whereas hemlock stems are smooth and streaked with purple.
2. Hemlock stalks are bulky and blackened near the bottom.
3. The parsnip leaves are longer, narrower and less toothed than those of the hemlock.
4. Water parsnip leaves grow as singles whereas hemlock leaves **always** grow in pairs or triplets.

Water parsnip stalks are tall, slender, strongly ribbed and grow two to six feet high. They must **never** be harvested until after you have learned the differences between them and water hemlock.

Use only the roots. Boil them until tender. You can overcome the problems of identification by a careful study of the plants. Learn the difference because water parsnip roots contain a vast amount of nutrition and make an excellent survival food.

Wild carrot (*Daucus carota*) also known as Queen Anne's lace

Found throughout North America in swamps, wetlands, sloughs and wet meadows. Wild carrot, when young, is identified by whitish flower clusters which are flat and very lacy with, usually, a single purple flower in the center. As the plant grows old it develops into a cluster which looks very much like a bird's nest as it begins to take the shape of a semi-globe. Roots are white and smell like a domestic garden carrot. The stalks are very hairy and grow to heights of two to four feet. Boil the roots after they have been sliced like garden carrots.

Medicinal use: The seeds can be used as a tea for the treatment of chronic coughs due to colds, hiccups, dysentery and colic. Pioneers, woodsmen and Natives used wild carrot tea when they had a touch of jaundice. It is also a good aid in digestion.

Warning: Use only the root and the seeds. Early plants resemble poison hemlock so check the stalks. Carrot stalks are **extremely** hairy whereas poison hemlock stalks are smooth and completely hairless.

Wild onion (*Allium cernuum*)

Found throughout North America growing in valleys, on hillsides and high up mountains. It grows six to twenty inches tall, has green, tall, grasslike leaves, small flowers with six petals are white to rose in color and smell like onions. All species are edible. Tender leaves and bulbs can be eaten raw or boiled, but are best used as a flavoring for fish and meats.

Warning: There is a poisonous plant called the death camus (*Zigadenus venenosus*) which looks like a wild onion. The flowers tell the difference. Camus flowers do not droop and do not have six-petalled flowers. They grow in a large cluster and are upright. The flowers are greenish or blue. Do not select wild onions unless the flowers are out (June to August).

Wild parsnip (*Pastinaca sativa*)

Identified by its tall (two to five feet), sturdy, grooved stalk, headed with five-petalled yellow to gold flowers which cluster as tiny umbrellas on up to fifteen stalklets. The leaves grow in pairs on either side of their stalks, except the top leaves which are usually triplets. Found throughout North America in open spaces. The roots, smooth and fleshy, are tasty when boiled until tender.

Warning: Wet or sweaty skin, if in contact with the leaves, will likely break out in a rash. The rash intensifies when exposed to sunlight. This rash, which has symptoms common to poison ivy, can last for months and be very itchy.

Wild potato vine (*Impomoea pondurata*)

A trailing vine with many single leaves all of which are heart shaped, it has large two- to four-inch white, bell-shaped flowers with pink to purple centers. The root is large and deeply buried and is found only in southern parts of western U.S. in dry fields. Boil, steam or bake after neutralizing the bitter flavor by several boilings.

Warning: Do not eat wild potato root in its raw state as it is a purgative. This trait is neutralized, along with the bitter flavor, only by boiling.

Summing up

It is very important that the characteristics of plants, i.e., hairy roots versus smooth roots, ribbed stalks versus unribbed stalks, whether fruit has seeds or not, etc., be understood by anyone who is in a survival situation. It makes no sense whatever for a person to survive for a week, then die because he forgot to check for the differences between a cattail root and a water hemlock root. Learn the differences and you will not go wrong. It does not take a botanist to realize that a plant that smells and/or tastes terrible is not edible. Pioneers, woodsmen and trappers who could not write their own names learned the differences. North American Indians had no written language and had no idea of either the plants' components or their scientific names, but they knew which were good and which were not. Anyone can learn to tell the good plants from the bad. The trick is to survive long enough to learn those differences.

6 Identifying Poisonous Plants

The best rule for choosing food plants for survival is to know the poisonous plants because all others are edible. It is essential for your good health to be able to positively identify the ones which are poison. Besides, it is easier to learn about the ninety-one poisonous plants than it is to try to remember the many hundreds of beneficial plants. For that reason this chapter is devoted to the plants which you **must** avoid at all costs.

The dangerous plants of North America fall into three discernable groups:

a. those which **will** kill you,
b. those which **might** and,
c. those which cause rashes if brought into contact with the skin or eyes.

The a. and b. groups cause illnesses ranging from death to mild or severe gastric upsets. An example of the—fortunately small—first group is the water hemlock. It is so deadly that even a small mouthful will kill almost immediately. Those of the second group, which contains about twenty-four varieties, are not always fatal but cause distress, often severe, of a gastric or neurological nature.

The distress caused by the c. group range from mild to severe rashes or blisters to temporary or permanent blindness. The latter two groups, some sixty-six plants in number, cause skin rashes or stomach and digestive tract upsets which will last from several hours to several days.

There are really only two main rules to follow when dealing with wild plants: (1) learn to recognize and avoid the common poison plants, and (2) there are no foolproof tests for determining the toxicity of a plant, including nonpoisonous ones.

The reason for this is simply because people vary so widely in body chemistry. What is beneficial to one is not necessarily good for another. Nuts are a prime example. Most people eat nutmeats with no ill effects while others cannot tolerate even the most casual contact. This is proven by the numerous cases of nut-based allergies which affect humans. As a rule of thumb if you are allergic to **any** nut developed for commercial use, e.g., peanuts, walnuts and hazelnuts, you **must** avoid wild nuts, including pine cone seeds. If you are not allergic to nuts or their by-products, e.g., peanut butter, peanut oil, etc., then wild nuts will not likely bother you.

Several abundant plants which are identified in this book as poisonous can be eaten under certain circumstances. Skunk cabbage is one such plant. It must be listed as poisonous, however, as in its raw state it causes troubles. Also there are several plants which have poison leaves and/or stalks, bulbs and flowers while the roots are completely edible. The wild parsnip is one such plant. Other plants have poison roots while their leaves, stalks and berries are edible. These are identified and described in Chapter 5. Care must be taken in how you prepare and cook these unique plants.

Fortunately, almost as if Mother Nature intended to give us fair warning, most poisonous plants generally appear ugly and unappealing, produce a fruit that is bitter and unpleasant to the taste, or grow from a root that would repel a ghoul. Do not think because you see an animal eat a plant or berry, the plant is edible. The digestive systems of animals and birds are unlike that of humans.

The following list contain the names of plants known to be internally or externally poisonous. If indicated by an asterisk (*) the plant is on record as having caused fatalities:

Internally poisonous:

American bittersweet (*Celastrus scandens*)
Anemone (genus: *Ranunculaceae*)
Apple-of-Peru (*Nicandra spp.*)
Arnica (*Arnica montana*)
Arrow arum (*Peltandra virginica*)
Arrow-grass (*Triglochin spp.*)
Atamasco-lily or Easter lily (*Zephyranthes atamasco*)
Azalea (*)(*Kalmia latifolia*)
Balsam apple or bitter gourd (*Momardiea charontia*)
Baneberries (*) (*Acteae rubra* and *A. alba*)

Black locust (*) (*Robinia psuedoacocia*)
Black henbane (*Hyascyamius niger*)
Bloodroot (*Sanguinaris canadensis*)
Blue flag or wild iris (*Iris versicolor*)
Blue cohosh (*Caulophyllum thalietroides*)
Bouncing bet (*Saponaria officialis*)
Buckthorns (*Rhamnus spp.*)
Buttercups (*Ranunculus spp.*)
Butterfly-weed (*Asclepias tuberosa*)
Canada moonseed (*) (*Menispermum canadense*)
Castor bean (*) (*Ricinus commonis*)
Celandine (*Chelidonium majus*)
Cestrum or Jessamine (*Cestrum nocturnum*)
Chinaberry or white cedar (*Melia azedarach*)
Clematis (*Clemantis spp.*)
Common tansy (*) (*Tanacetum vulgare*)
Corncockle (*Agrostemma githago*)
Cowbane or water hemlock (*Cicuta manaduta*)
Daphne (*Kalmia spp.*)
Death camas (*Zigadenus gramineus*)
Devil's bit (*Chamaelirum leteuus*)
Dicentras (*Dicentra eucullaria*)
Dogbane (*Apocynum spp.*)
Elderberry (*Sambucus nigra*)
Ergot (*) (*Claviceps spp.*)
False hellebore (*) (*Veratrum viride*)
Fly-poison (*Aurianthum muscaetoxicum*)
Fool's parsley (*Aethusa cynapium*)
Four-o-clock (*Mirabilis jalapa*)
Foxglove (*) (*Digitalis purpurea*)
Goat's rue (*Tephrosia virginiana*)
Golden club (*Orontium aquaticum*)
Golden-seal (*Hydrastis canadensis*)
Ground cherries (*Physalis peruviana*)
Holly (*Ilex verticillata*)
Horse chestnuts (*) (*Aescelus hippoeastanam*)
Horse-nettle (*Solanum carolinense*)
Horsetail (*Equisetum arvense*)
Hydrangea (*Hydrangea macrophylla*)

Jack-in-the-pulpit or Indian turnip (*Arisaema triphyllum*)
Jerusalem oak (*Chenopodium botrop*)
Jimsonweed (*) (*Datura stramonium*)
Lantana (*) (*Lantana camara*)
Larkspur(*) (*Delphinium spp.*)
Lobelia (*Lobelia spp.*)
May-apple (*Podophyllum peltatium*)
Mistletoe (*) (*Phoradendron flavescens*)
Monkshood (*) (*Aconitum napellus*)
Mushrooms (*) (*Agaricus meleagris spp.*)
Nightshades (*) (*Atropa belladonna*)
Poison hemlock (*) (*Conium maculatum*)
Pokeweed (*) (*Phytalacca americana*)
Prickle poppy (*Argimone albiflora*)
Rattlebox (*Crotalaria spectabilis*)
Rhododendron (*Rhododendron spp.*)
Scarlet pimpernel (*Anagallis arvensis*)
Scotch broom laurel (*) (*Cystisus scoparius*)
Skunk cabbage (*Symplecarpus feotidus*)
Snow-on-the-mountain (*Euphorbia marginata*)
Spurge (*Daphne mezereum*)
Star of Bethlehem (*Orinthogalum umbellatum*)
Water hemlock (*) (*Cicuta macalata*)
White snakeroot (*) (*Eupatorium rugosum*)
Wild indigo (*Baptista tinctaria*)
Wild cherries (*) (*Prunus spp.*)
Wild lupine (*Lupinus perennis*)
Wisteria (*Wisteria frutescens*)
Yellow jessamine (*) (*Gelsemium sempervirens*)

Externally poisonous (cause stings and rashes):

Eyebane (*Euphorbia maculata*)
Nettles (*Urtica spp.*)
Poison oak (*Rhus toxicoterendron*)
Poison sumac (*Rhus vernix*)
Poison ivy (*Toxicodendron radicans*)
Spurge nettle (*Cridoscolus stimulosuis*)

Trumpet creeper (*Campsis radicans*)
Wild parsnip (leaves) (*Postinaca sativa*)
Wood-nettle (*Laportea canadensis*)

All nettles are edible when boiled as soup or tea. The root of the wild parsnip is edible as a vegetable and can be eaten either raw or cooked. Do **not** touch the leaves with wet hands or a rash resembling poison ivy will occur. Unlike poison ivy, which generally clears up within a week or two if you can avoid scratching the affected area(s), the rash caused by the leaves of wild parsnip, scratched or not, can remain painful for months. All parts of poison ivy and poison oak are poisonous. Surprisingly, there are people who are totally unaffected by either. They can roll in the stuff, hold it in their hands and rub it all over their arms without a thing happening...no one knows why.

If you or anyone in your group should eat a poisonous plant quick action is needed. Immediate vomiting should be induced and then the victim **must** continue to drink large amounts of water and repeat the vomiting procedure until the stomach is totally clear of all the poison. If the victim is unconscious there is little you can do except keep him or her as comfortable as possible. Artificial respiration may work and should be employed to keep the victim breathing. If the victim is convulsive keep him or her restrained as gently as possible until the victim settles down. Even if the poison should not prove fatal, the victim will probably be in a great deal of discomfort—possibly for days after.

The lists above indicate all known poisonous plants but not all will be identified in detail. The reason for the omission is that so many poisonous plants resemble others of their species so closely that if you know one you will recognize the others of the same family. It is also well to remember that in addition to looking unattractive, many poisonous plants have a bad odor. Some exude an obnoxious sap which tends to encourage avoidance. Others are so rare that it is unlikely you would ever see one. (When dealing with plants in the wilds never gather those which cannot be harvested in a usable abundance.)

Some of the plants listed are found nowadays near towns and other inhabited areas (the horse chestnut and the American yew, for example, are deadly poison but are, as yet, rarely found in the wilds). They are listed here as an added precaution against those which have escaped into the bush, a phenomena increasing yearly as cottagers try to spruce up their summer residences with domestic plants. Seeds travel on the winds for miles and birds eat the fruits of plants then expel the seeds in their droppings. Many of our so-called wild plants are not native to this continent although to see their numbers you would never know it. A great number of plants were brought over by Vikings, while others were introduced by explorers long before the first settlers arrived.

Identifying Features of Poison Plants

American yew (*Taxus canadensis*)

An evergreen shrub which grows three to ten feet, it has flat, pointed needles (1") which are green on both sides. It produces a juicy, red, open berry that contains a single, hard, yellow, visible seed. It is found in moist woods throughout Canada and in the U.S. to a line parallel to the southern border of Virginia. Birds, particularly the northern mockingbird, eat the seeds, but they are poison to people. This plant contains taxine, a heart-depressing drug.

Atamasco-lily (*Zephyranthes atamasco*) also called stagger-grass, swamp lily or Easter lily

Found in wet woods and clearings, the flowers are quite large and shaped like daffodils. They are usually white or pale pink and the leaves are smooth and waxy. While its bulb looks like an onion, it has no odor. This plant has been mistaken for edible because of its similarity to the daffodil and the domestic onion. However, the flower has a musty, cloying smell. The plant grows to a height of one or two feet and is found in clearings and wetlands. So far, it is strictly a U.S. plant found mainly in the southeast, but is spreading. The plant is to be avoided.

Note: This lily's odor reminds most people of a funeral parlor. If you are unsure the plant is a lily, smell the flowers. You will readily know why they associate the lily to the funeral parlor. It is the smell of death and you would be wise to remember that if you decide to bite into a lily bulb.

Baneberries (*Actaea rubra*)

The flowers of these plants, whether scarlet red or white, have a small black spot at the center. This spot gives baneberries it alias of the Doll's-eye plant. Leaves are large and divided with saw-tooth edges, flowers are bushy and elongated and appear at the end of a long, leafless, smooth stem. The white baneberry grows on a thick stalk while the red baneberry has a thin stalk. Both grow to a height of one to two feet (35—70 cm). All parts of a baneberry plant contain a poisonous glyocide. Even a few berries will cause dizzy spells which will be followed by violent retching, and the roots are no-less toxic. The Latin name indicates it is a severe laxative. Indian shamans extracted the oil for just that purpose.

Blue flag (*Iris versicolor*) also called Rocky Mountain iris

Very similar in appearance to the domestic garden iris. They grow two to three feet (70 cm—1 m) in height and are found in swamps and wet meadows. Do not misidentify wild iris as cattails or sweetflag because **all** iris species are poisonous. Iris roots taste extremely unpleasant and only a very hungry person would ever eat one. Indian shamans used the root to treat liver disorders, so it has medicinal qualities.

Bouncing Bet (*Saponaria officialis*) also known as soapwort

Stem and leaves are smooth, the stem is thick and jointed. Flowers are white or pink and grow in clusters. Its very showy petals are scalloped and sometimes double. It grows one to two feet high (30—60 cm), and is found in clear spaces. Bouncing Bet attacks and destroys red blood cells if eaten. The plant got its curious name because it was used to make soap and a "bouncing Bet" was a washer woman in pioneer slang. Some people have used the plant in the mistaken belief that the peas inside are edible because they resemble the common garden pea.

Buttercup (*Ranunculus acris*)

A familiar flower to most people, buttercups contain a poison which causes intestinal irritation if eaten. The leaves and stalks can blister the skin. The flowers cause no problems but have no known use.

Butterfly-weed (*Asclepias tuberosa*)

A member of the milkweed family with erect clusters of yellow-orange flowers, its stems differ from edible milkweeds as they are rough and hairy and its juice is watery. The plant will grow one to three feet high, and it has seedpods which grow upright and are four to five inches in length. Edible milkweeds have smooth stems and a thick milky product. Avoid butterfly-weed as it has none of the edible qualities of its family.

Canada moonseed (*Menispermium canadense*)

A climbing vine, it is woody and has green stems that twine. Leaves are five to ten inches (12—25 cm) long. They are circular with a pointed tip. Drooping flowers are white and produce large, soft, black grapes. It is this feature that makes the Canada moonseed so dangerous as some lost souls have eaten the fruit thinking it to be wild grape. Each fruit contains one flat crescent-shaped seed and the fruit is very bitter. Canada moonseed grows in moist woods, along streams and in thickets.

Common nightshade (*Solanum dulcamara*)

Bushy weed that grows upright to a height of 1 to 3 feet (30 cm—1 m), throughout North America in open areas. Flowers have five petals and yellow anthers which resemble tiny beaks. Its fruit is an unattractive black berry. Its Latin name indicates this plant is related to tomatoes, potatoes and egg plants but it has absolutely none of its cousins' qualities.

Dogbane (*Apocynum androsaemifolium*)

It grows on dry hillsides close to the edge of woods. Plants branch and have paired oval leaves. Stems are reddish and flowers are white or pale pink, bell shaped and exude a noticeable fragrance. The stems exude a milky juice. Dogbane plants have slender stems which grow one to four feet (35 cm—1.3 m) tall. The flowers produce pods which grow in pairs to a length of three to eight inches (7.5—20 cm).

Dwarf larkspur (*Ranunculaceae*)

This larkspur has loose clusters of small blue or white flowers with five to seven petals, and is similar to the buttercup. All larkspurs are poison and can be fatal in large quantities. They are best left alone. While not profuse in Canada they grow in abundance from Minnesota to Pennsylvania and have escaped to secluded adjoining areas of Ontario and Manitoba.

Fox glove (*Digitalis purpurea*)

A pretty plant often found in a place of high honor in domestic rock gardens. It is another of the many plants introduced by pioneers to this continent several centuries ago. Brought over as a source of medicine it quickly escaped into the wilds. It has tall, hairy, erect stems and the flowers spiral in vertical growth with up to eighty blossoms and come in pink, white or purple shades. This plant is the source of *digitalis* and the entire plant is extremely deadly for those who do not know how to use it.

Goat's rue (*Tephrosia virginia*) also known as wild pear

Its long, narrow stem has fine, white, silky hairs and has leaves which are feathery, narrow and untoothed along the edge. It has white flowers which resemble pea blossoms and grows seedpods which are long, flat and hairy. Inside the pods are green peas which look as if they might be a good substitute for the real item. **They are deadly.** Plant grows in sandy woods and open spaces.

Ground cherries (*Physalis spp.*) also called husk tomatoes

A smooth plant, it is three to five feet tall (1–1.6 m) with diamond-shaped leaves that taper into stalks. Flowers are yellow with a purple throat. Fruit is red or purple. The fruit can be eaten if it is **very** ripe. However, the risk is not worth taking. Unripe fruit and the plant's leaves are always poisonous. Ground cherries are somewhat rare.

Jimsonweed (*Datura stramonium*) also called Jamestownweed

Contains a narcotic similar to belladonna. All parts of this plant are extremely toxic. Identified by large, three to five inch (7.5—11 cm) trumpet-shaped white or pale violet flowers. The leaves are very coarse with uneven edges. Both plant and flowers exude a vile scent.

This weed grows to a height of two to five feet (70—150 cm). It is related to the domestic tomato and potato, and for that reason has been misused from time to time by lost persons who thought it could be eaten. It grows in waste areas throughout most of North America.

Monkshood (*Aconitum napellus*) also known as aconite and wolfsbane

Monkshood is relatively rare in Canada but prevalent throughout mountain regions of the eastern U.S. It grows two to three feet (70—95 cm) in height. Has large, pretty, cowl-like flowers of blue or white. Two anthers hang down like tiny mustaches. As a result the entire flower resembles a small face peering out from under a hood, hence its name. Found in low woods and on damp hills. This plant is poison in its entirety and one taste will cause troubles. Its poison is the deadly aconitine. Indian shamans knew how to use this plant as a sedative. Monkshood is called wolfsbane in western areas.

Mushrooms and toadstools (many species)

With the exception of puffballs the size of basketballs, which are easily identified, stay away from mushrooms unless you know what they are. Puffballs are edible, can be eaten raw, fried or dried for future use. Sliced and added to stew or soup, it adds taste and vitamin quality. Select only very large puffballs, however, as what you think are small puffballs may be an immature, and very deadly, mushroom called death's angel (*Amanita phalloides*).

Poison hemlock (*Conium maculatum*)

A plant of many branches and hollow stalks which have grooves and purple spots, it has a most unpleasant smell when the stalk is bruised and the roots reportedly taste terrible. The root is similar to that of the wild carrot. It is found from northern Canada to the mid-U.S. Even small amounts will cause paralysis and can prove fatal. The similarites to wild carrot are striking, but the poison hemlock has a completely hairless stalk and that is what to watch for. Wild carrots have very hairy stalks and are edible.

Poison ivy (*Rhus radicans*)

This prolific plant is usually a vine that trails or climbs, although it is sometimes found as an erect shrub. The leaves grow along trailing stalks which are four to fourteen inches long and are variable so they can be glossy or dull, smooth or toothed, but all are hairy to some degree. Leaves always grow in clusters. The plant grows berries which are hard, white and hang in drooping clusters. This plant causes extreme rash which is itchy and painful, and scratching spreads the rash. The rash is somewhat treatable with mud and/or baking soda. Apply crushed jewelweed for best results.

Poison oak (*Rhus toxicoterendron*)

The effects of a run-in with this plant are similar to poison ivy. Treatment is the same. Poison oak grows as a bush, always erect with hairy leaflets lobed like an oak leaf. It is found throughout North America.

Poison sumac (*Rhus vernix*)

Poison sumac is a tree with leaves up to twelve inches long. Each leaf has up to thirteen smooth leaflets. Twigs are hairless. The bark is smooth with black spots. Ivory white berries droop from the branches. Sumac grows to about twenty feet tall and is found in wooded swamps from Canada to Florida. Avoid touching this plant as it is more virulent than poison ivy. **Note**: All other sumacs can be used for teas, but unless you can recognize these species leave them **all** alone. Nonpoisonous sumacs have red berries.

Rattlebox (*Crotalaria spectabilis*)

A hairy plant, quite small at twelve to fifteen inches (35—45 cm) in height, it produces seeds in black pods. When dry the seeds within rattle, hence the name. Some authorities claim the seeds make a fine substitute for coffee but until further data is available the plant is best left alone. The raw seeds are unquestionably highly poisonous and it is debatable if boiling crushed dry seeds will remove the toxins.

Water hemlock (*Cicuta maculata*) also called spotted cowbane

Very tall (3—6 ft. or 1—2 m) with a purple-streaked stem with branches, this hemlock has many clusters of dirty white flowers clumped closely together. Found in wetlands and swamps, this is

Bear berry, aka kinnikinik: An excellent survival food as it can be eaten directly from the plant. Note the green, paddle-shaped leaves. They can be dried and used as tobacco. It is nicotine-free. The berries are not all that tasty but are packed with nutrients.

Painting: National Archives of Canada, the Hans Ludwig Blohm Collection, ref. no. 1924-080.

Buffaloberry: Similar to bear berries. Edible but quite tasteless. Makes good tea.

Photo: National Archives of Canada, Hans Ludwig Blohm Collection, ref. no. 1924-080.

Burdock: The entire plant, except the burrs, is edible. Young leaves can be eaten raw but old leaves must be boiled in several changes of water for at least thirty minutes. Note the furry underside of the leaves below.

Photo left: Derrick Ditchburn.

Photo below: Gil Bailey.

Cattail: One of the world's greatest survival foods due to its versatility and abundance. Cattails in winter are fine for emergency rations. Pare the heads and stalks to the tender centers. In March, when the ice begins to melt, many tender new shoots will appear below the water level. These can be harvested and eaten with no special preparation. See Chapter 8 for the best method of using cattails and bulrushes.

Photo: Derrick Ditchburn.

Chickweed: Its tender, juicy, pale-green stems reach about a foot in length. Flowers are small, white and star-shaped with five petals. Leaves eaten raw together with cooked stems make a great two-course meal.

Photo: Gil Bailey.

Clover: A versatile food as the leaves, flowers and seeds can be used as tea, boiled greens or flour. It is rich in protein.

Photo above: Nancy Miller.
Photo right: Derrick Ditchburn.

Cow parsnip: Similar to hemlock, which is deadly poison. Eat only mature plants. Peel the stems and leaf stalks and boil.

Photo: Derrick Ditchburn.

Kelp: Loaded with vitamins, iodine and potassium. When cut into short strips, boiled in fresh water and left to infuse, it produces a rich, aromatic liquid that can be used to cook fish or small animals in a stew.

Photo: Nancy Miller

Juneberry, also known as Saskatoon berry: Can be eaten uncooked straight from the bush. Filled with vitamin C.

Dandelion: An exceptional emergency food because leaves, flowers, stems and roots all have their uses. Roots when dried, make a good coffeelike beverage.

Labrador tea: The leaves remain on the plant year-round, making it the perfect source of survival food. Drink Labrador tea during the first few days almost exclusively as its nutrients will keep you going long enough to search out and gather other, more filling plants. *Photo: Derrick Ditchburn.*

Reindeer moss: Use only plants that are silver-gray or ashy. Never use yellow or green-gray plants. Boiling the entire plant will produce a thick soup. Note: All lichens are purgative. Soak in several changes of cold water for six hours before using. *Photo: Jim Pojar.*

Mint: All mints make good tea. An excellent digestive aid and a great soother for stress.

Photo: National Archives of Canada, Hans Ludwig Blohm Collection, ref. no. 1924-080.

Oyster plant, also known as salsify: The flowers show from dawn until midday when they close up. Roots can be boiled as a food or dried and crushed as a coffee substitute.   *Photo: Derrick Ditchburn.*

Pine trees: The tree ranks high as a survival food. It produces tender needles, an edible inner bark which can be powdered into flour and it supplies cones in abundance (see inset). Note: Anyone allergic to nuts must avoid pine seeds.

Photos: Nancy Miller.

Plantain: A top-flight emergency plant. Young leaves may be eaten raw while the broadest leaves can be used as bandages. As they are mildly astringent, they will help in the healing of open cuts and wounds.

Photo: Nancy Miller.

Rock tripe: Use it as a boiled vegetable or add it to soup or stew. All lichens must be soaked for minimum of six hours but rock tripe requires at least eight hours.

Photo: National Archives of Canada, Hans Ludwig Blohm Collection, ref. no. 1924-080.

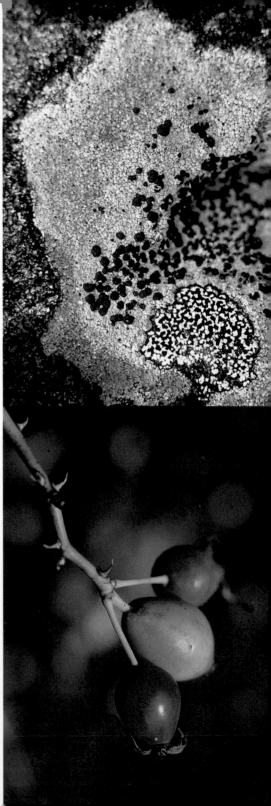

Rose hips (right): Use boiled as food. Makes great tea and syrup. You can live for months on rose hips alone if need be.

Photo: National Archives of Canada, Hans Ludwig Blohm Collection, ref. no. 1924-080.

Skunk cabbage (below): Good only as a last resort medicinal plant and should be avoided as food unless absolutely nothing else is available. Never eat the leaves either uncooked or cooked before thorough drying, because chemicals within the plant produce an intense burning sensation in the mouth and throat.   *Photo: Nancy Miller.*

Sting nettle (above left) and Thistle (above right and below): All thistles and nettles are edible except the burrs and flowers. Most have stinging qualities. Roots do NOT sting, so pull from the ground by the roots. Stinging qualities dissipate by boiling.

Spruce trees: The traditional Christmas trees; like the pine tree, their needles and bark can be eaten. The pitch, when removed from the tree's crevices, can be chewed. Spruce needles or pulverized bark can be simmered in water and used as an effective cough syrup.

Photo left: Nancy Miller; inset: Province of British Columbia Ministry of Forests.

Water parsnip: Resembles hemlock so do not harvest them until after you have learned the differences between them and water hemlock. Only the roots are used.

Photo: National Archives of Canada, Hans Ludwig Blohm Collection, ref. no. 1924-080.

Pink Fawn lily: All colored lilies have edible tubers. Avoid white lilies as they are poison.

Photo: Derrick Ditchburn.

Water lilies: Edible tubers. New flower petals can be brewed into tea.

Photo: National Archives of Canada, Hans Ludwig Blohm Collection, ref. no. 1924-080.

Wild carrot: In winter it can be used as emergency food. Easily recognized by the way its flowerless clusters tend to form into a rough imitation of an old bird's nest.

The plant on the right is a product of the past summer so the bird's nest effect is not very pronounced. Next year it will be bigger and closely bunched. Use only first-year growth like this plant.

At the end of the stalk is a frozen root. Dig it out and boil it. It makes an excellent emergency food. While it will be tasteless and starchy, a few of these roots will supply a good amount of vitamin C and other minerals. *Photo: Author.*

Wild onion: It has green, tall, grasslike leaves and small flowers with six petals that are white to rose in color and smell like onions. Do not confuse it with the poisonous death camus which looks similar. Camus flowers do not droop and do not have six-petalled flowers. They grow in a large cluster and are upright with greenish or blue flowers. *Photo: Derrick Ditchburn.*

Sumac: In winter or summer it is actually best left alone, but in a pinch those with red clusters like these can be used for a healthful tea. Never use sumac with white berries or those that have drooping clusters. In winter the species of sumac shown here is easily identifiable by its mossy branches.

Photo: Author.

Sedum: Edible as tea or as boiled leaves and stems. Plentiful in North America.

Photos: National Archives of Canada, the Hans Ludwig Blohm Collection, ref. no. 1924-080.

★P Red baneberry, also called the doll's-eye plant: They are easily identified by the circular black spot which adorns each berry. This identifying mark is also found on the white baneberry. Both of these plants are deadly poison. *Photo: Province of British Columbia Ministry of Forests.*

★P Buttercups: Contain a poison which causes intestinal irritation if eaten. The leaves and stalks can blister the skin. The flowers (not shown) cause no problems but have no known use.
Photo: Nancy Miller.

★P Toad stools: These look pretty but are deadly poison. Avoid all toadstools.

★P Hemlock: Note the dirty flowers and smooth stems. Look for purple streaks near the bottom of the stalk.   *Photos: National Archives of Canada, the Hans Ludwig Blohm Collection, ref. no. 1924-080.*

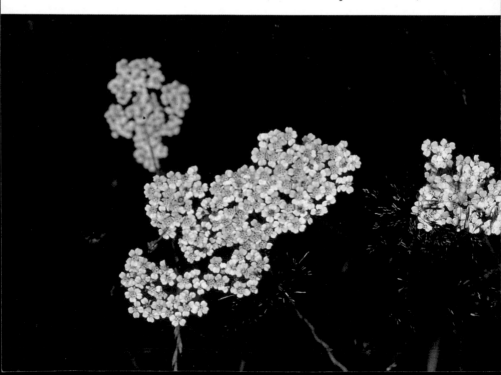

North America's deadliest plant. One mouthful will kill speedily but with great distress. Water hemlock (WH) differs from poison hemlock (*Conium maculatum*) in that hemlock acts more speedily than WH and is more or less nonviolent. Hemlock was favored in Ancient Greece as the method of execution for respected citizens convicted of political or morals crimes. Socrates became one of its more famous victims when he chose execution by hemlock rather than permanent exile following his conviction by an Athenian court on morals charges.

Whereas poison hemlock gives a quiet death by slow paralysis, WH kills with cramps, convulsions and much pain. Only the brain remains unaffected until the final minutes.

Wild indigo (*Baptista tinctaria*)

The plant has blue-gray to green-gray leaves and stem, with yellow flowers loosely clustered on ends of multibranches. The plant will grow to three feet and is found in dry woods and clearings from southern Canada down a line bounded by the states of Minnesota, Iowa and Missouri to Louisiana then east into Florida. The young shoots resemble asparagus but must be left alone. They have been known to poison cows, but there is no record of human deaths.

Summing up

The best rule to follow in avoiding poisonous plants is to leave anything alone that you cannot recognize as being of the edible variety. Stay strictly within the varieties of the edible plants described in Chapters 5 and 7 and you will not go wrong. For the first few days of isolation stay **exclusively** with cattails, bulrushes, water lilies and dandelions. As the days pass you will get a much better idea of what you can identify easily.

7 Medicines and Treatments

Before you use advice from this chapter read Chapters 5 and 6 which deal with plant recognition.

Regardless of where you find yourself, Mother Nature provides for your convenience a pharmacy of abundance. Spider webs make a good bleeding stopper—but you will need a lot of webs. Gather enough fresh, clean webs (early morning is best) so you can make a pad big enough to cover the wound entirely. It doesn't have to be thick—an eighth of an inch will suffice. Place it over the bleeding wound and cover with a cloth or plantain leaves. Secure the webs and cloth tightly enough that they will remain in place. The spider silk will usually congeal the blood quickly. Repeat the procedure the following morning if the wound still tends to seep. Once the bleeding has stopped for good, remove the matted spider silk and wash the area. Cover with plantain leaves for another day or two.

Plantain (*Plantago major*)

The broad leaves of the plantain contain a mild astringent which helps to close wounds. Bruise the leaf and place it directly on the wound. Leave in place for about two hours. Replace the old leaf with a fresh one as required. Use as often as needed as the agent in this plant is mild and wears out quickly. When a scab begins to form, remove the coverings and let the air complete the healing (see Chapter 5).

Willow

The common drug called aspirin is actually acetylsalicylic acid (ASA). It is found in the roots of white willow trees and the bark of spirea bushes. Both grow everywhere in North America. The spirea bark produces a fine powder when crushed. One method used is to crush the bark with rocks in the fashion of a grist mill. It is a time-consuming chore but the resultant powder can be of great benefit to relieve minor pains when taken with cool water.

Good results can be obtained by chewing a piece of willow bark. Do not use this method for a toothache, however. For some reason it only makes it worse. It reacts in the same way as does an aspirin tablet when held against an aching tooth. The ASA draws the moisture from the tooth which dries the dentine (the pricipal mass that makes up the tooth, similar to bone) and causes the pain.

There are also small amounts of ASA in the resin of spruce and birch trees. This residue is found on the outside of spruce trees and can be chewed like gum or boiled. Spruce needles make an ASA tea if you boil green needles in a cup of water for twenty minutes. Remove the needles, let the liquid sit for five minutes, then sip the tea. Strips of the outside bark, when boiled, also produce an ASA tea.

A word of caution about ASA: do not overdo the dosage as too much can cause stomach pains. A very small amount of fresh powder is usually sufficient to alleviate minor pains while an eight-ounce drink of tea will generally resolve the problem.

Chickweed (*Stellaria media*)

See Chapter 5 for a description on this plant as it is edible as well as medicinal. For medicinal purposes it is effective on boils and cankers. Boil large amount of chickweed for five minutes. Drain off the water and allow the chickweed to cool only enough that it can be applied to the affected area without undue pain. Keep pressed against the afflicted area until the chickweed cools. Apply this treatment three or four times a day and within three days you should have some good results.

Chufa (*Cyperus esculentus*) also known as nut-grass

This plant is a sedge related to bulrushes and it grows nearly everywhere. The tubers have the medicinal value of being a great digestive aid. Soak the tubers two days in cold water (your stream will suffice), simmer until the chufas are tender. Dry for one day then eat like peanuts.

Jewelweed (*Impatiens capensis*) also called wild touch-me-not

This medicinal plant has a tremendous range being found from Nova Scotia right across to the west coast in Canada, from Alaska south to Oregon and along the eastern seaboard to Florida. Whether it has food value or not is still undecided, but there is no disputing its value as a medicine against the rash of poison ivy and poison oak. It may also work against thistles and nettles and may even be useful against insect stings but nothing is definite on this. Tests at the University of Vermont some years ago found jewelweed contains 2-methoxy-1, 4-naphthoquinone, a crystalline agent. The Vermont scientists announced this is why jewelweed is so effective as an anti-itch medicine.

Tender, fragile stems with many branches are light green in color. Leaves vary from extremely tiny at the base to three inches long near the top of the plant. Leaves are egg shaped with pointy tips. They are serrated along the edges. The plant gets it name from its waterproof condition. Rain stands on the leaves in round drops and, when light reflects from these droplets, they sparkle like diamonds.

Jewelweed has pretty, yellow flowers which produce seedpods about three-quarters of an inch long. When the pods are ripe, they split suddenly if touched, giving it its secondary name. The pods snap open with an audible popping sound, curl back and toss the seeds a fair distance. There can be some entertainment value in this for the survivor if he/she has an hour to spare; and nature would be helped as well. Do not hesitate to stroll through a patch of jewelweed brushing against the plants along the way.

Skunk cabbage (*Symplecarpus feotidus*)

If you develop a bronchial or catarrhal condition with the attendant cough, skunk cabbage may be the best remedy. Cover one ounce of **dried** root with boiling water and steep for thirty minutes; strain. Take a small amount (about one tablespoon) three times a day. This treats bronchial and other bad coughs effectively, and has good results when used for hacking night coughs. Indians used this medicine for centuries and it worked well for them. Try wild carrot seed tea first as it is safer. If it doesn't work, try the skunk cabbage remedy, however it must be thoroughly dried. Drying can be done by hanging over a fire or hanging from a branch during hot weather. (Skunk cabbage is described to greater degree in Chapter 5.)

Wild lettuce (*Lactuca canadensis* and *L. scariola*)

These plants grow all over North America. *L. canadensis* is abundant, is native to North America and is also called horseweed and tall lettuce. *Lactuca scariola* is also called prickly lettuce and compass plant. This equally abundant plant is an escapee having been brought over from Europe by early settlers.

L. canadensis thrives in low places and in meadows from east to west and north to south. *L. scariola* prefers the higher ground. Either can be used as a medicine. Break or cut one of the tall seed stalks. A thick, white milk exudes which soon coagulates into a rubbery substance. Over a period of hours and days this substance will turn a brownish color but remains usable. Chew the rubber in small amounts for relief of pain. Because it is a very mild sedative, it will help insomnia as well.

Summing up

There are many hundreds of plants which provide various forms of medicines. Many plants, such as foxglove and mandrake, contain very effective drugs. Natural drugs, however, unless you know how and when to use them, can be a potential danger. If you need a medicine to aid your digestion, alleviate a headache or other pain, or if you simply feel the need to alleviate anxiety, stick to the recommended plants described above and to the teas described in Chapter 5. They work and will cause no ill-effects. Use when needed.

A few more medicinal uses for plants will be found in the chapters on recognition. The vast majority of edible plants contain vitamin C, the great scurvy fighter. Others also contain A and some contain E. Usually, the plants you eat as food will also supply the medicinal qualities that go along with them, although some lose these qualities in cooking. A good diet of edible plants will keep you healthy.

In the long run, because survivors usually suffer only from minor illnesses, the teas made from catnip, wild strawberry leaves, peppermint and spearmint, in that order, will probably solve your problems better than inducing the medicinal qualities of other plants—and will require less work and bother.

8 Insect Pests

There are in the woods of North America any number of obnoxious insect pests, and most are easily recognized. Use mud or clay to treat and reduce swelling caused by insect stings or hornet, wasp, blackfly and horsefly bites. If you are camped beside a stream, check closely to determine the type of soil the banks are made of. This inspection will give you an edge in case you need it. If you are really lucky the soil will be a heavy, grayish clay; and clay has a number of uses besides treatment of bites and stings. It can also be used for baking meat (see Chapter 13). If clay is not available, scoop mud from the creek bottom if it is of a thick texture. Make a mud pack and smear it **thickly** over the sting or the bite. Let it dry. It will help keep the swelling down while the minerals in the mud provide a healing medicine. This is also an excellent remedy for nettle stings, poison ivy and poison oak rashes.

Abide by the premise that an ounce of prevention is worth a pound of cure. It stands to reason that you should avoid being stung or bitten.

Throughout North America are mosquitos, deerflies, horseflies, blackflies, midges, which are very tiny pests northern Indians call "no see'ems," and gnats. Along with bees, wasps, hornets and other insects with attitude, these pests can make life miserable. In order to keep them at bay you will need an effective repellent. If you do not have any (or have run out of store-bought oil) you will have to make your own. (Musk-Oil and Deep Woods are two very good commercial brands. Be sure to follow directions. Do not splash the oil in your eyes and keep out of the nose and ears. Many repellents use DEET [a chemical which confuses the insects' sensor antennae and spins them out of control] as a base. These repellents keep bugs at bay but they have a tendency to melt plastic so it is difficult to forecast how your skin will react over prolonged use of the product.)

The best natural repellent is smoke. It is free and easily made. Build a small fire. Cover the flames with green boughs. Red cedar is very good as its smoke is oily and thick. When the smoke starts to form, stand in it. The idea is to make yourself smell as smokey as possible. Keep your eyes closed, though, as the smoke will irritate them. Make sure you get a good amount of smoke. Turn around slowly several times over twenty minutes or so. You may have to smoke yourself several times over a couple of days but eventually it will take effect. Smoke is effective against mosquitos which, if you let them, will drive you crazy. The stories of lost hunters and trappers going insane from mosquito attacks are not legends or myths. They are true.

A good repellent, but without doubt the most repulsive mixture in the world, is one which Natives of the far north have used for centuries. If you catch a fish leave it to rot. When it begins to smell sufficiently deplorable, rub it on your outer clothing. Then go stand in the smoke. The combination will keep anything away. As revolting as this substance is, it is highly recommended for use during May and June in areas of high blackfly infestation—northern Ontario, northern Saskatchewan, Manitoba and northern Alberta. Anyone who has lived through a heavy infestation period of blackflies will tell you that nothing is worse than the flies—not even the repellent.

In the evening, when mosquitos are generally at their worst, sit or work so the breeze will cause the smoke from your fire to waft around you. All flying insects hate smoke.

Ticks

Smoke will not help one bit against ticks and if you are in an area of heavy brush the chance of tick infestation is greatest. Ticks are arachnids (in other words, a species of spider) and resemble mites, only ticks are much larger. They spread Rocky Mountain spotted fever, tularemia (rabbit fever), relapsing fever, cattle fever and Lyme's disease, all of which can be deadly. Tularemia is also caused by eating infected rabbits so if you snare a rabbit check its body closely for tick sores. Discard the rabbit if you see tiny ulcers on the outer skin.

If you become infected by a tick bite early symptoms will be nausea, inflammation of lymph nodes, headache and high fever. Nothing short of expert medical attention can be done about this and it will either pass or not, depending on the individual's constitution.

Prevention of tick bites is easier than trying to find a cure. Keep your trouser legs and sleeves closed tightly at the wrists and ankles.

Keep your collar buttoned tightly. If you notice that a tick has landed on your skin do **not** brush it off. By the time you see or feel it, the thing will have its head burrowed into your skin. If you brush it off the head will remain and your troubles will begin.

First, do not panic. If you are near your campfire heat a stick or knife blade and hold the hot end very close to the tick. The heat will cause it to wriggle out of its burrowing position whereupon it will fall off. If it persists move the heat closer. No heat? If you have any alcohol or **hot** water put a drop on the tick and it will react in a similar manner as it does to heat. When the tick drops to the ground kill it.

Leeches

Leeches are longish annelid worms, round or slightly flattened, with segments externally divided by secondary rings. They are usually black and have a suction disk at each end of the body. They are found in lakes, rivers, ponds, creeks and streams near shore where the water is still, stagnant, brackish or swampy. A very few species live on land, even fewer in the sea.

The hot stick is also the best way to dislodge leeches which may attach themselves to your legs with what will seem to be a death grip if you enter water where they abide. Hold the heat close to the leech and it will quickly fall away. Do not kill leeches as they are useful creatures and should be protected. Return them to the water. Leeches will never cause you harm other than draining off some of your blood. In fact, leeches were used by shamans for centuries (and by doctors of medicine as far back as medieval days) as treatment for blood disorders and high blood pressure. Modern physicians and surgeons, not famous for embracing old ideas, are returning to the leech for the old treatment of blood-letting (using leeches to drain blood from patients to cure, fevers, heart problems, aches, etc.) so there must be something of good in it.

Leeches do not carry disease of any type. The objectional part of a leech is its personality. People panic, quite needlessly, when they discover their legs covered with the little horrors. If you discover the leeches while still in the water simply brush them off. Once out of the water, however, the heat treatment is best.

Hornets, wasps and bees

The yellow jacket hornet, the Viking of the wasp family, was introduced to North America by early settlers. Heaven alone knows why. Because they are not native to this continent they have no natural enemy to keep them in check. That is why they are so plentiful.

This particular species of hornet will generally leave you alone unless you start swatting at them. Wasps of all types are excitable but the yellow jacket is the "berserker" of the species. Make them angry and you are in for major trouble. If you keep your distance they are unlikely to even notice you, but if one should come close, stand still and avoid sudden movement. One, perhaps two, may come in for a closer look but consider the ordeal a character builder and a severe test of self-discipline and remain still. Once you are deemed to be no threat the hornet(s) will leave.

If you find yourself in a situation where hornets have decided to attack there are only three things you can do. If you are near deep water, hurry into it and keep your head under as long as you can. Swim underwater until you are clear of the area. If you are not near water, head for your campfire and stand in the smoke. If you were wise beforehand and equipped your lean-to with a front cover as illustrated in the chapter on shelter building, go there. Do not reemerge until the hornets have gone.

If you discover that you have built your camp near a nest of hornets or wasps—move your camp. It is much easier to relocate the camp than to dispossess the hornets. Hornet nests in the wild differ alarmingly from the ones you see in towns and cities. Bush nests can be huge and house many thousands of these insects. The same applies to bee hives. Bees are generally docile, and sting only when frightened, grabbed or in defense of their hive. Bees will not normally attack anyone. The African strains lately found in parts of the southern U.S.A. are a different story, however. If you find yourself lost in any state south of 40° N latitude, assume any bees you see are of the African strain and go out of your way to avoid them.

If you are attacked by swarming bees head for deep water, while a second choice can be smoke. It is not known how smoke affects African bees, but one would assume they do not like it.

If you are stung, mud packs or baking soda work well on common bee stings. Very little research has been done under the conditions a lost person will find himself in with African bee stings, but they are likely treatable by the ordinary methods. When you are trying to survive you must try everything so go with the mud first then try baking soda and hope for the best.

Horseflies and deerflies

Horse and deerflies both produce painful bites with the horsefly's being the worst. Also, its bite mark is more prone to fester than that of the deerfly's. Use a mud pack or soda on the bite. Smoke is the best repellent. A horsefly (genus *Tabanidae*) is twice the size of an ordinary housefly, is dark brown and has light stripes along its body. Its bite is extremely painful, as painful as any wasp bite. Swatting is the best weapon against it should it get close enough, but two or more hefty swats will likely be required to kill it. Do not swat until you have a good chance to knock it down—and do not miss. Horseflies get every bit as angry as yellow jackets. An angry horsefly can be a difficult opponent. Fortunately, they are solitary insects so there is little danger of being caught in a swarm.

Deerflies are reddish brown and smaller than horseflies. They have a sort of fur which resembles deer hide, hence the name. Normally they won't bother humans but they do have an annoying habit of buzzing in for a look-see. They do bite so keep out of their way as much as possible. A good swat will kill a deerfly. Mud deals nicely with its bite. Jewelweed is also an excellent medicine for stings and bites.

Most insects, such as gnats, moths and common flies (rare in forests) are annoying but harmless. Gnats will swarm around your head and are nothing but annoying. They appear during the last light of a hot day's evening. Moths are harmless night insects attracted to light. Several species are very large with a wide wingspan and these often look extremely fierce—but they are all completely harmless. Keep the fire low and they will never bother you. All flies and hornets are attracted by garbage so if you keep your campsite clean they will be less of a bother.

It is worth repeating that a littered campsite will also attract bears, wolverines and raccoons so for your own safety and peace of mind, keep it clean. Some of the smaller black bears are often not all that unfriendly but their advances must be discouraged. The first reason is that a small bear may appear friendly but he is always extremely dangerous. The second reason is that once such a bear locates your camp and finds it to his liking, he will never leave. The best way to discourage wild animals is to keep the place clean and tidy—and, while not appearing hostile, do not give the impression that you are friendly.

9 Snake and Spider Bites: Prevention and Treatment

Highly recommended: Anyone planning to travel through snake country should carry an antivenom kit. They are available at pharmacies at reasonable cost.

Although most North American snakes are harmless, a great many people are deathly afraid of them. People lost in the woods are advised to adopt that attitude. Unless you can recognize the different varieties of snakes it is best to avoid them all.

If you are bitten by a snake there are two certain ways of knowing if the snake is venomous or harmless. The first is by the bite. Venomous snakes puncture the flesh with **two deep fang marks** one or two inches apart. Harmless snakes (garters, bull snakes, king snakes, etc.) are not fanged and rarely get agitated enough to bite. If they do, because they have tiny teeth, they will leave a row of tooth marks.

The second sure way of knowing is that venomous snakes pack a wallop that has been described by some as feeling as if a hot poker was driven into the pit of the stomach, while some others say it is akin to being hit with a solid right hook into the solar plexus. Either one is guaranteed to get your immediate attention.

In North America a number of areas are home to poisonous snakes. Some are extremely lethal while others are of lesser potency. Lesser potency means only that if the bite is untreated a severe fever will ensue and death will be fairly slow. Whether the snake that bites you gives forth slow or quick poison you must treat it—quickly—because in neither case are the end results likely to differ.

Central Ontario is home to a venomous snake called the massissauga rattler, a hissing cousin of the eastern diamondback. It is about three feet long and its markings are mottled greenish brown in color.

Because it is very shy it is hard to spot. Furthermore, it never goes looking for trouble. However, its strike is as quick as lightning and its venom packs a punch. However, the poison moves slowly enough to allow reasonable time for treatment.

Southern Alberta, Montana and southern Saskatchewan provide homes to two rattlesnake species called the western diamondback and the prairie rattler respectively. Both are larger than their eastern cousins but are no less deadly. The poison from these snakes affects one fairly quickly.

The Okanagan Valley, the arid inland area of Washington and B.C.'s Thompson River Valley harbor the deadly timber rattlesnake (*Crotalus horridus*), a version of the diamondback snakes. It also has fast-acting poison. The eastern rattlesnake (*Crotalus adamanteus*) is the eastern version of the timber rattlesnake.

Washington State, Montana and North Dakota share the rattlesnake population with B.C., Alberta and Saskatchewan as snakes simply will not recognize borders.

Kansas and the other prairie states in the U.S. are home to the ground rattlesnake (*Sistrusus catenatus*). It is somewhat rare and small—only a foot or so in length— and it also has diamond shapes on its back.

Rattlesnakes may be encountered in any hot, desertlike environment. Because they are cold-blooded, which means their bodies are effected by the environmental temperature, snakes have a hard time surviving, which may account for their dispositions. They spend most hot days seeking cool places, usually the shade under large rocks and in thick brush, and cool nights under flat rocks to take advantage of stored heat. Stand too close to or stick your hand under a rock or reach into or kick at a stand of underbrush and you do so at your peril.

In the southwestern U.S. you can also encounter rattlesnakes: the diamondback (largest of all North American species) and the sidewinder are quite common. The sidewinder's trail is easy to spot if the terrain is sandy or dust-covered. This is because the sidewinder travels sideways so its tracks appear as a series of S shapes lying on their sides in the sand. Old west cattle brands employed such an S which cowboys called a "lazy S."

A rattlesnake of any type is easily recognized. When the tail is shaken the rings rub against each other to produce a sharp "buzzing" sound. These are the so-called rattles. They also resemble pit vipers—head wide at the base and narrow at the nose. Pit vipers are a species of snake that give the world the cobra, the asp, the adder and a few others. The "pit" in pit viper comes from the indentation, or pit, on each side of their somewhat triangular head. The bodies end in a series of loose, dried skin rings.

Rattlesnakes are predominately brown with a variety of tones ranging from light olive to greenish brown. Venom is transferred through two upper front fangs. One should remember that a snake cannot lunge beyond its own length which will give you an idea of how close you can safely approach. Remember, though, they strike faster than the eye can follow and may move closer if annoyed. It is always best to leave the area to the snake. He was there first and will not easily relinquish his turf.

No snake is the archetype of rapid mobility (top speed is only about three miles per hour) and they will not take a deliberate run at you; but neither will a snake tolerate intrusion into its hard won territory. Rattlers will **sometimes** sound a warning before striking, so you should keep an ear open when in certain places. But, do not count on a warning. The old tale that a rattler will always sound a warning is simply part of their mythology.

The flesh of any snake is edible and of excellent taste when cooked properly. Remove the rattles and the head—be careful to avoid being scratched by the fangs. Skin the snake, remove the flesh in filets. Cook on a spit over the fire or on a flat rock. It tastes every bit as good as chicken. Snake meat is **not** poison. Only the venom can harm you. Save the skins as they can be useful later.

If you are hiking in the U.S. deep south—specifically Florida and Louisiana—and become lost in a swamp or bayou, the poisonous snakes are chiefly two species of the coral snake and the water moccasin, also known as cottonmouth. These, the deadliest snakes in North America, have extremely fast-acting venom. They are never found outside the southern states in natural habitat because of climatic conditions.

The coral, or harlequin as they are sometimes called, are a cousin to the cobra of Asia except they are not hooded. A fully grown coral is about two-and-a-half feet long, has a small blunted head and a body ringed with bands of red and black with narrow bands of yellow on either side of its back. An equally lethal member of the species, called the sonoran coral, is found in New Mexico and Arizona.

The cottonmouth is larger than the coral and not brightly skinned. Found in swamps and everglades it is as much at home in the water as it is in the trees which overhang the waterways. (Incidentally, rattle-snakes are **also** adept at tree climbing.) When walking along a swamp trail always keep one eye on the water's edge and the other on the branches above. Although a cottonmouth's venom is probably faster acting than that of the coral it is a moot point, as in either case survival is unlikely without an antivenom kit.

Some eastern states are home to the copperhead (*Agkistrodon mokasen*). It is two to three feet long, and has a copper-colored head. Its body is brown with hourglass shapes of chestnut hue on its upper body. Its underside is pinkish white with dark spots. The copperhead's bite is lethal but the venom does not act as quickly as that of a rattlesnake. Treatment, nonetheless, must still be quick.

Self treatment for a snake bite is painful, messy and never easy. Neither can it be guaranteed. From the moment of the bite you must remain as still as possible. Activity will only hasten the flow of poison. Make haste slowly is the best advice because a snake bite is no occasion to start running around in circles wondering what to do next. Every second counts and you will face few emergencies as great as being bitten by a poisonous snake.

First, you must slow the flow of blood to the heart and brain. The easiest way to achieve this is to apply a tourniquet tightly about four inches **above** the bite. This is the only time that you should disregard the advice that tourniquets are not recommended as a first-aid device. Remember, however, that prolonged application will certainly do harm. However, it has its good side in the case of snake-bite.

Whether you use a tourniquet or not, your only priority is to expel the poison. Forget those stupid tales wherein you cut an X across the bite and suck out the poison. That only worked in old Hollywood B-movies and Zane Gray's western fiction.

If you have rum, brandy or another drinkable alcohol available, use it. Pour some on the wound and also on the blade of your knife to reduce the chance of infection. Then take a good slug of it yourself. It will help you in the forthcoming ordeal.

Retie the tourniquet (your belt will suffice) about six inches above the bite, tighten as much as possible. Carefully cut a half-inch, horizontal incision at points an inch or two **directly above and below** the bite. The incisions should only be deep enough to allow free bleeding but not so deep to sever nerve endings or sinews. The theory behind this is that the flowing blood will take much of the poison with it. Loosen the tourniquet to allow the wounds to flow freely a minute or two, then stop the bleeding by using **direct** pressure. A cloth or plantain leaves can be used to soak up the blood.

Still applying direct pressure to the wounds, retighten the tourniquet a minute or so then loosen it and release the direct pressure. This will allow the blood to flow again. Let the flow continue for another minute. Repeat the entire process several times before stopping the blood flow completely by direct pressure. Remove the tourniquet and continue the direct pressure until the blood stops.

You will not get all the poison out of your system, but what remains will hopefully be insufficient to do more than cause a fever—albeit perhaps a high one—and a period of extreme weakness. Fever can be curtailed with ASA and/or immersion in the cool water of a stream or lake. With luck the fever will pass within three days, although you will remain very weak for several more. This is another reason to establish a base camp and make a shelter and gather some food for reserve during your first days of being lost.

Spiders

Rattlesnake country is also black widow spider country. Her zoological name is *Latrodectus mactans*; the first part means "secret biter" which pretty well describes her true nature. (Part of her myth is a vexatious habit of slaying her mate as soon as he has fertilized her eggs. This is not an automatic conclusion for the hapless male. The black widow will often allow her mate to scurry away. However, should he foolishly decide to hang around for some pillow talk and a bit of afterplay, he is doomed. He must be very swift from the onset or he will definitely end up wrapped in silk and put aside as a late lunch.)

There is no need to fear the males of this species: they are wimps in every way. Only the females bite. Black widows inhabit grass clumps, rock crevices, decaying trees, old, run-down cabins and sheds. They often spin their webs under the business part of outdoor privies, so be careful in those places. The old buildings of ghost towns in the hills of western states and provinces are natural habitats for black widows. That old cabin you might find and think to be a good shelter may be crawling with widows. Check out the nooks and crannies before you settle in.

These spiders are easily identifiable by the red hour-glass shape on their underside. This insect packs a nasty bite which releases a venom of four, slowly moving poisons. It is the fourth poison that can kill a human. The poison is not considered sufficient in wallop to prove fatal to a healthy adult though it can kill a sickly one. It can certainly kill a small child.

The black widow's bite is extremely painful. It has been described as like being pierced with a red-hot needle. Within seconds the area becomes red and begins to throb. An intense pain then spreads toward the center of the body. The thighs, then the shoulders and finally the back become painful. After a short while the abdomen area becomes as stiff as a board. The pulse weakens, skin becomes clammy, breathing gets difficult and the mind grows dull. Shock and paralysis follow in severe cases. The entire ordeal will last two or three days—and you will either die or survive.

The real danger in any spider or insect bite lies when scratching or poor care of the bite area allows blood poisoning to develop. Blood poisoning is usually fatal without proper treatment.

People with known allergies to spiders, bees or other insects who contemplate venturing into the woods, should **always** include as part of their survival kit the antitoxin kits available at low cost in drug stores. If you are going to hike in snake country, the same suggestion applies.

The first thing to remember in case of black widow spider or venomous snake bites is **controlled haste**. The less time wasted the better the chances of recovery.

Scorpions

Scorpions are secretive creatures for the most part and are not a problem in northern zones of North America, but can be in southern areas. They all look alike, but range in size from one inch to eight inches. All produce venom through a tail stinger. The venom causes rash, swelling, discoloration of the area, dizziness and/or fever. Few stings are likely to prove fatal to a healthy adult, though most can kill a child.

The exception to the norm is a native scorpion of Arizona. A particularly nasty creature called the Arizona scorpion (*Centruroides scupturatus*) is the most poisonous insect in the state. This scorpion grows to eight inches in length and is hairy. Like all scorpions it is segmented, has eight stubby little legs and two large, sightless eyes which protrude from the top of a tiny head. Because it cannot see, it cannot attack its prey by taking a run at it. It "hunts" by stinging **anything** that ventures within a few inches of it—and the accuracy of its stinger is wondrous. The venom, a combination of two nerve poisons, quickly paralyzes the victim's body and then stops the heart. The venom is produced by two glands which supply the stinger at the very tip.

This little horror is not an endangered species by any means. It is found throughout the state and thrives in abundance along the bottom of the Grand Canyon. It is especially numerous in the area around Phantom Ranch. Its sting is quick and deadly. Anyone contemplating a hike in the Arizona hills, desert, outlands or the Grand Canyon should never travel without an anti-venom kit made specially to reverse the venom of this animal. The Arizona scorpion's venom puts that of the diamondback rattler to shame.

Scorpions spend their time in brush, caves, under rocks, in decayed trees, under boards in old cabins (avoid old mining claim sheds, etc.) and they hide in rock crevices. Hikers and lost persons who bed down for the night in scorpion country should take care that sleeping bags are kept tightly closed at the neck. Stuff your socks tightly into the tops of your boots before retiring for the night. Give the boots a thorough shaking every morning before—and after—removing the socks. Small scorpions have an annoying habit of crawling into boots and sleeping bags during the cool nights.

If you should wake up to see a scorpion staring at you, do not panic. Remember it cannot see you, but if it is within a few inches you will have to—and be very quick—roll **away** from it, three rolls should be about enough. Do not stand up first—just roll until you have put about ten feet between you and it.

Summing up

Avoid all snakes unless you know the species you have come across. Nonpoisonous snakes have teeth in rows. Poisonous snakes have two fangs on the upper jaw. All snakes are edible. Avoid scorpions. Even the small bark scorpion gives a nasty sting. Spiders should be avoided. Even harmless ones can produce a painful sting. If you are planning a trip into snake, spider or scorpion country take an antivenom kit with you. Planning may save your life.

10 Group Survival Means Teamwork

Nowadays when an aircraft goes down in bush or forest country it is nearly always found and more often than not there are survivors. Sometimes it is found that those who initially survived the crash died later because those who might have helped couldn't deal with the problems which arose during the first few days.

As in small planes, there is often no discovery for at least seven days because even the largest planes can be hidden by a hostile forest. In 1949, a four-engine passenger aircraft carrying fifty passengers and a crew of six crashed during a scheduled flight from Winnipeg to Vancouver. Searchers scoured the terrain for more than two weeks. The plane was not discovered until 1994 when, quite by accident, hikers came across it. Whether anyone survived the initial impact is unknown. The forty-five years that had elapsed had wiped out all the evidence of what had transpired following the initial impact.

A group is any number from four people to 200 or even more. Group survival is very different from individual survival for a variety of reasons. First, a single survivor makes all his own decisions. Second, one person does all the work. Survival is dependent on individual initiative, labor and the will to live. Groups, on the other hand, must share both initiative and work which means everyone must work together toward the same end. This is easier said than accomplished as there will always be divergence of opinion; and in very large groups there is always one or two who will be too bone lazy to shoulder any part of the task at hand. These are also those prone to chronic complaint. These types are usually more annoying than anything else and are usually the first to succumb to the various pressures.

A prime detail is the one of who will be the group leader. In the case of plane crash or wrecked ship, whether the craft is privately owned or commercial, the captain or pilot retains the same authority he held before the mishap—and that authority must be recognized and never questioned. If the captain is killed—or too seriously injured to retain command—authority automatically passes down the line, by rank or position, to the other crew members. Thus, the final leader of the group may well be a seaman or a flight attendant. **Regardless of the position a crew member holds, his or her authority is final unless it is relinquished to a passenger more experienced.**

The same rule applies to any group which starts out on a hike or excursion under the leadership of one particular person—such as a trail guide. That person remains in charge so long as he or she is capable of exercising the authority previously vested.

However, in some cases circumstances will show that another has the expertise, experience or leadership qualities which dictate that he or she take overall charge. No captain, pilot or leader in his right mind will ever refuse to relinquish authority to such a person if it is in the common interest. Likewise, no one in a group who knows he or she has those qualifications should ever fail to step forward. Survival time is no time to be either shy or stubborn.

Once leadership is determined, either by right of crew status, appointment by the captain or election by the group, he or she must take immediate charge. The first task should be to divide the group into small units.

The size of the units should be determined by the total numbers. A unit up to twelve persons can be managed nicely. Partners and friends should be kept together as should families. Each unit should delegate **one** person to be the unit leader who shall work closely with the group leader. The group leader in turn should keep the unit leaders apprised of his wishes and ideas. The unit leaders in turn will keep the units knowledgeable of what is happening. These delegates can make tough going a lot easier.

The group leader should immediately survey others to determine who among them holds particular skills. Some must be appointed to aiding and attending to the injured under direction of whatever medical persons may be among them. Even a basic first-aid course qualifies the recipient to hold the position as the medical expert under the circumstances.

Members of fishing and hunting clubs should be deployed in determining the presence of wild life; and be responsible for catching same. Anyone with knowledge of plants and herbs should be made responsible for the identification and gathering of same. The group leader should canvas the survivors in case one of them might know the art of navigation. Military personnel or members of a cadet corp might be present. These people often possess the knowledge of fixing location by sun or stars which will determine the longitude and latitude. This information then can be relayed via cellular phone if one is among the collected material.

Everyone has a role to play and it is up to the leader to bring out the best in everyone. Small children must be cared for and comforted, the elderly must be seen to, the campsite must be kept clean (preteen children are ideal for this) and berries and roots must be gathered (teenagers do a good job here). The list is so long that every person, including those with injuries, can be kept busy.

Work must begin as soon as possible. What remains of the plane must be salvaged. All supplies, blankets, baggage and other equipment should be removed and sorted. Nowadays, the likelihood that there may one or more cellular telephones is greater than ever. These should all be checked to determine which, if any, survived the impact. Only one at a time should be used in the interests of conservation. Remember, also, that although a cellular phone might allow you to make contact with someone miles away it will be of little use in directing rescuers unless you can tell them where you are. Meanwhile, the leader and those delegated to positions of lesser authority must keep the others working. Work is absolutely necessary, not only to assure the plane's equipment is utilized to the fullest, but to maintain morale. It is a fact that busy survivors are happiest when they have no time to dwell upon what might be their fate. It is of utmost importance that everyone remain as busy as possible over the first days. A good leader will see to this important priority above all else.

Once the injured are treated, the dead must be removed from the immediate area. Shallow graves should be prepared some distance from the place where the leader decides the campsite should be located. Interment is necessary to keep scavenging animals away and to prevent—or at least minimize—the chance of sickness befalling the ranks of those who remain. Illness is something the entire group must strive to avoid.

Shelters must be assembled. Lean-tos are best because they are quick to assemble and are efficient. Each unit should have its own fire and keep its own water if it is abundant, but food must be shared from a common larder.

The group leader should select a storekeeper with great care as this person must oversee the rations and moderate the almost inevitable squabbles which will occur. Rations for some of the injured and those engaged in the heavier work may have to exceed those of others. The storekeeper must be prepared to explain the reasons. The group leader must also be ready to explain why those engaged in more taxing work are getting more than others. This is a matter which often leads to misunderstanding and must be handled properly.

The group leader and his delegated subordinates must be prepared to rule with firm hands, and all involved would be well advised to tread cautiously. It is advisable that everyone obey the group leader even if a decision or two may seem unreasonable. Compliance is important because, following rescue, there will in all likelihood be an inquiry. Should the authorities be informed, or even suspect, that troubles had beset the group each person will be required to explain his or her conduct and actions—or lack of same.

Rebellion against a crew member or other authorized leader will likely be viewed by a board of inquiry as the civilian equivalent of mutiny. Moreover, defiance of an elected or appointed leader would likely be viewed by the board in the same light. Indeed, there is little doubt it would, especially if the group leader's decisions had been the chief reason for the survival of the group.

Summing up

The key word in group survival is teamwork which means simply a spirit of equal sharing and mutual cooperation. Without teamwork the entire group may well perish. The forest, tundra or desert is no place for petty disagreements or clashes of personalities. The group leader's word is law and should be so considered.

11 Snares, Spears and Traps

It is an unfortunate fact of life that a massive search will be conducted only for a period of between seven and fourteen days. If the survivor is not found within ten days the search is scaled down. After two weeks it will in all probability be discontinued. This chapter, therefore, is intended for those who, having been in the bush for more than nine days, feel their chances of being found are not as good as they were a few days previously. For starters, unless you really think you have a good chance of finding a settlement of some sort, staying put for another couple of weeks may be best. Ultimately, it is up to the individual, and whether you decide to walk or stay put, some planning is involved.

Either way you will require a food supply for the future and that is where meat comes into the picture. Small and medium-sized animals, precooked, plus a supply of roots and plants which can be carried are the answer to the problem of walking out. If you stay, hoard a small supply of cooked animal meat to augment the plants you have located.

Small and medium-sized animals are best caught through the use of snares, preferably of copper wire although twine can be used for squirrels. A properly made snare, one with a free-running noose, will kill quickly or at least keep pain and suffering to a minimum. Wire of any variety is good but copper wire is best because it is a soft metal. Copper bends easily into a slip knot that will not loosen, break or kink, most other wires are too stiff. Twine, acceptable as a tree snare, is **not** suitable for ground use as it can break or be chewed through, allowing the animal—and hence your supper—to escape.

The easiest animals to snare are tree squirrels and rabbits, in that order. They also taste better than woodchucks or other ground animals, although porcupine is certainly tasty. **However, be sure to check all rabbits for tick bites** (see Chapter 8).

Squirrels

We will deal with tree squirrels first because they are easy to snare. This is because they are basically stupid. The trees in which they live have higher IQs. Squirrels follow set patterns in their daily routine of leaving and returning to their nests. They are also lazy and take shortcuts whenever the opportunity presents itself. Work these weaknesses to your advantage.

Be watchful for squirrels. They will be there but you have to be quick to see them. Do not waste your time with the so-called "flying squirrels" (genus *Glaucomys*) as they are near impossible to catch, although with intense patience, they can be induced to approach and accept food. Some, over time, can become fairly tame. With the exception of the flying squirrel, who has intelligence, squirrels are pretty well the same. Concentrate on them.

Although you will see squirrels which appear to be of several varieties they are generally all of one species. Their only differences are in color—some are gray, some are black, some are red and some are multi-colored. You will see the occasional black or gray squirrel sporting a bushy red tail. That simply means his mother was a bit of a sport.

As you observe the squirrels, you will notice they run up and down trees head-first whereas most animals with the ability to climb (porcupines, raccoons, bears) go up head first, but descend rump first. You will also note squirrels spiral the tree as they go up and down. This trait makes snaring difficult and this is where you bring trickery into play:

Step 1. Choose three or four saplings about twenty feet high. A diameter of two to six inches is best. Cut them down and trim some branches. Leave the bark intact.

Step 2. Lean the saplings against trees you know are home to squirrels. Secure the thickest end into the ground. Leave them alone for a couple of days and watch. Within a day or two you will notice squirrels have begun to use the saplings as shortcuts up and down the trees. If the squirrels shun them, move the saplings to other trees.

Step 3. Make four or five snares for each sapling by following the directions in the diagram. Loop the snares around the saplings at distances of two to three feet and secure tightly.

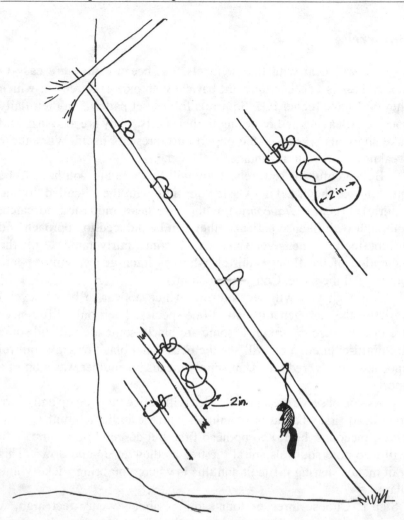

Squirrel snares (fish-line string).

Place the "running" loops **on** the saplings so they rest lightly. The reason is that you want them to snare the squirrel by the neck and then topple off. This will ensure the squirrel dies quickly and as humanely as possible. Survival is a grim business but it need not be cruel.

As noted above, squirrels are not the brightest animals in the woods. Once they start using the saplings as shortcuts they will continue to do so. The fact that their relatives are dangling in snares will not deter them one iota. They will simply run past without a second look.

It is a good idea to rig five or six trees in this manner to ensure a continuous supply of squirrels (For methods of cooking see Chapter 11).

Rabbits

Rabbits are only a little smarter than squirrels; and they are bigger so the meat supply is better. One rabbit will suffice for two meals whereas with squirrels about four per day are needed. A snare for a rabbit needs a running loop of three-inch diameter with the other end secured **very** tightly. The best way to do this is to fasten the other end to a stake driven well into the ground. Or you can tie it to a tree.

Rabbits are found by locating their "runs." These are little trails through grass and are not very hard to spot because they are indented in the undergrowth. Rabbits generally go directly from point A to point B in a fairly straight line.

Rabbits, like squirrels, are creatures of habit and they follow the same run every day. Place your snare loop across the run, about two inches above the ground. Placed thusly the rabbit will be caught by the neck and, if the noose is properly slipped, will die quickly. If it is caught by the foot the rabbit may chew it off. There is no reason to be the cause of an animal's suffering, so do the job properly and it won't happen. The loop should "float" but not sway enough to warn the rabbit that it is there.

Place a second snare at least twenty feet further along: two will do. To place any more may defeat the purpose by tipping the rabbits that something is amiss. While they are not particularly brilliant (the sight of one or two of their brothers caught in snares is unlikely to trouble them), three bodies will definitely tell them that danger lurks.

It is best to trap two or three runs at a time but limit your diet to one rabbit for two meals (a large jackrabbit is worth three meals). You won't need any more to provide yourself a healthy amount of protein. If you catch two rabbits, cook both. A cooked rabbit will keep at least three days if kept in a cool place. It is a good idea to keep a reserve as there is no guarantee of catching an animal per day. (The cooking of rabbits is covered in Chapter 13).

The Woodchuck or groundhog

Whether you know these little marmot-type rodents as ground-hogs, ground squirrels, pasture poodles or woodchucks, they are one and the same. They have dark brown fur, are about fourteen inches long and weigh about five pounds. They do not taste very good but are edible in an emergency. They live in the ground, are very shy and scamper underground at the slightest movement or as each and every shadow passes over them. They can be caught only with a sturdy wire snare. Place a snare with a noose of four inches directly across the mouth of the burrow. Secure it very tightly because these little creatures are wiry and strong. Be certain the animal is dead before you remove it from the snare because their front teeth cut like a straight razor. Make sure the wire is secure because if the animal gets back into his burrow you will never get him out. Gut and skin the carcass and boil the meat gently for two or three hours.

Traps for Long-term Survival

Traps are for large animals such as deer, elk and moose. They must be used only by a person who has come to the realization that he is not going to be found for a very long time and will have to spend at least a few months, probably an entire winter, in isolation. Once that realization settles in and you know you are going to become a more or less permanent resident of wherever you are you **must** begin to think in terms of long-term survival. This is an unpleasant situation to contemplate but it has happened to others and a good number of them managed well enough. If you do end up in this situation and decide to trap large animals, remember when you are eventually rescued to ensure that you destroy all active traps or inform your rescuers where the traps are located so they will be able to take them apart.

The Apache deer trap

Named after a method of trapping used by the Apaches of the American Southwest, the Apache deer trap is nothing more than a ditch covered with twigs. Because it is designed to break the animal's front legs it is a cruel procedure. Its operation, however, is simplicity itself.

A deer will usually leap over low obstacles in its path rather than go around them, so the trap must be placed where it will produce the best results. It requires hard work and while it definitely works its use is distressing to most people.

Step 1. Find a narrow trail frequented by deer. This will require careful dawn and dusk observation. During the day, look for tracks or signs of fresh deer droppings.

Step 2. Place brushwood barricades about two feet high across the trail or place two fallen trees in such a way that they block the trail. Watch to see if deer jump over them as they proceed on their way. If they do, you have set the first part of a two-way trap. If they go around the trees, lower the obstacle; however, the higher you can get your deer to jump, the better the trap will work. Once you get them leaping the obstacles check to see where their front feet touch down. **This is very important**.

Step 3. Now the hard work starts. You must dig a trench across the trail. This trench must be at least two feet deep by eighteen inches wide and must be centered where the deer's front feet touch down after he leaps the barricade. By placing barriers correctly, you can utilize one trench to get the deer from either direction. Cover your trench loosely with small branches, shrubs and grass.

Step 4. If all goes well, your deer will vault the obstacle, crash into the pit, break one or both front legs and be rendered immobile. (If neither leg breaks and he manages to clamber out and escape, your trap is finished as the deer will not use that trail again for a very long while. Dig another trench on another trail some distance away.) If, as you approach the trench, you see the deer is indeed trapped you must then do as the Apaches did. Quickly dispatch the deer with a spear. It is suggested you use a spear as they are easy to make and allow you to kill the deer while keeping a safe distance from his antlers. A pole (an inch in diameter) about eight feet long and sharpened at the end makes a good spear. Be as quick and efficient as possible as this is a cruel trap and is included only because survival is often cruel. You must consider yourself as being more important than the deer.

Step 5. For the preparation of the carcass, see Chapter 13.

Making a pole snare

Spruce hens, found mostly in forested areas of northern states and western Canadian provinces, are grouselike birds that roost in trees at sunset. They are skittish and flighty during the day but as daylight wanes they have but one thought and that is to find a branch and go to sleep. Once settled on the branch they are set for the night and that is when they can be caught. All that is needed is a pole and a snare which must be made of wire. String is useless as it is limp and cannot be made to slip over the head of a bird. Wire is rigid and does the trick.

Watch for the birds as they begin their roosting routine. Once they settle on their branches, pick out two or three that look plump and watch them closely. Take a lesson from cougars and wolves: once you have chosen your prey never, ever change your mind. Always stay with your original selection(s).

Be very patient and make no movement as you watch. Never approach, for they will spook and fly off. As dusk settles deeper the hens will become calm. At the very last light, just before the final darkness falls, when the shadows are well established and just before they tuck their heads under a wing for the night, sneak up behind the bird you have selected. Swing the pole up in front then quickly loop the snare around the hen's neck and snap the pole downwards and sideways. This motion will tighten the snare and pull the hen off the perch all in one motion. The snap should break the hen's neck. Quickness is necessary as you do not want to cause a fuss which will spook the others. Release the dead bird from the snare and repeat the procedure with a second bird and then a third. Three are all you need and will feed you nicely over the next few days—five days if you have caught a rabbit to go with them.

If you are adroit with your snare, the hens will remain unaware that you are a menace to their well-being and will continue to roost in the same trees night after night. If you botch it they will leave, and you will either have to find their new roosts or go without a tasty meal. Spruce hens are good but often have a flavor of pine needles. Old ones are more strongly flavored so try for younger birds.

To make your pole snare you need only a eighteen-inch length of wire and a pole of half-inch diameter and seven or eight feet in length. Use about eight inches of the wire to fashion the loop and the same to secure the other end to the pole. It is a good idea to make a small hole through the pole through which you can run the end of the wire before winding it around for security.

This type of snare can be used to pull a porcupine or a raccoon out of a tree as well. However, you will need a stouter pole (1–2 inch diameter), a wider noose and more care as either animal can put up a good fight.

Fishing nets and nightlines

Fish is an excellent source of vitamins, proteins and oils and will keep you well fed and healthy. Any fish in North America is edible including carp, mudcat and sucker, three fish generally shunned because they are "bottom feeders" and therefore considered garbage. Mudcat, a rough species of catfish lacking the fine texture of the true catfish also known as channelcat, is really quite delicious despite its ugliness. Carp, a staple food in Oriental countries, is very tasty when taken from cold-water lakes and streams. They are usually brown, have large scales and are unattractive to say the least. In warmer waters the flesh tends to be somewhat spongy and that turns most people off. Suckers, which are blackish gray, are not attractive either but when taken from cold waters are tasty enough. Besides, you are in no position to be fussy. The best way to cook these fish is by slow boil. Trout, salmon and others are best grilled on a hot, flat rock.

An ideal way to catch fish is with a gill net strung across a creek or river where the water is swift flowing but not rushing as in rapids. A gill net is best because it works day and night, leaving you free to do something else. A sturdy gill net is easily woven from string, crochet thread or fish line. The strings must be cut long—at least five times as long as the net you intend to make. You also need two sturdy ropes or very long, sturdy saplings (about half-inch diameter) for the top and bottom frames. The procedure for a net with a wood frame is the same as if using ropes.

Step 1. First determine the **width** you wish your net to be. A width of six to ten feet is generally sufficient. The width of your net should be twice its height.

Step 2. Take a length of twine, double it, loop over the upper frame a foot or so in from the left end. One inch to the right loop another doubled length of twine. Make sure you pull the loops as tight as possible. Repeat the procedure until all the

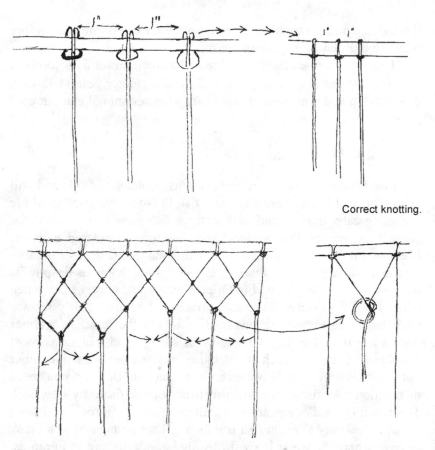

Correct knotting.

Three easy steps for constructing a fishing net.

strands are in place, two inches apart and hanging loose until a final double strand of twine hangs at the far right end about a foot in. The number of strings used will determine the net's width. These are the "original double strands" and will be referred to from here on as the ODS.

Step 3. Always work from left to right. Tie the **right** string of ODS #1 to the **left** string of ODS #2. Tie with a looped knot (see diagram). These two strings will become a double strand. Let it hang loose and proceed to the next ODS, the one on your right. Tie the remaining string from ODS #2 to the left string of ODS #3. These now will form a double strand which you will also let hang loose. Now tie the remaining string from ODS #3 to the left string of ODS #4. Continue in this manner until all the ODS are mated. A series of half-diamond shapes secured to the upper frame now extend in a horizontal line.

A new series of double strands hang loose. The one on your far left will be the starting point of row two. Repeat the process left to right, row by row, until all the strings are tied to others. The result will be a series of full diamond shapes, more or less equal in size and about two inches across, running the width of the net. Carry on in the above manner until all the strings are mated and there are enough diamonds to ensure your net will stretch across to the desired width. You will end up with a bottom row of loose strings. Tie these strings securely to the bottom "frame." Try to keep the diamonds uniform, your first efforts may be poor but keep trying. Expert tying does not come easy.

The diamonds should be two inches across in order to catch a fish of two or three pounds, the average size of a river fish in most places. If the fish are one or two pounds in size, the diamonds should be one to one-and-a-half inches. The diamond size depends on the size of the fish in the river and can easily be adjusted by retying the looped knots. Do not make the diamonds too big or all you will catch is a lunker which will likely rip the net to shreds. Making them too small, on the other hand, will catch only tiny fish (about six inches long) not worth the effort of keeping. Make the net as wide as you wish but a height of three to five feet is recommended.

To secure the net in the stream or river you will have to use your own devices as no set formula exists. In a river or wide stream use sturdy saplings imbedded securely in the river bottom. If your stream is narrow or has a bottleneck where the fish must enter, and you have plenty of rope, tie it into place using trees on opposite banks. A bit of experimentation is in order at this point. Whenever possible, use sturdy saplings as they free your rope for other important uses. One thing to remember is to set the net at or just below the water line and string it tightly.

As the fish pass into your net they will be caught by the gills. Small fish will pass through two-inch-wide diamonds, but anything of adequate size (one to three pounds) will be caught. Likewise, the huge fish (the one which will rip the net to shreds) will not likely enter. In their struggle to free themselves the fish, which are quite strong, will cause minor damage which will need constant repairing. Repairs are tedious and time consuming. However, if you hope to catch fish, you will have to allot yourself an hour or two each morning to make repairs.

The easiest method to make repairs is to untie the net from the bottom up as far as the damaged area then retie the strands. Another method is to weave a new diamond into the hole but that is never as strong as a proper repair. However, it will suffice for a time, depending on the catch and the size of the fish caught.

The art of net-mending becomes easy after a few repairs. If you remembered to include a large spool of fishing line in your pack you will have plenty of yarn for two or even three nets. Subsequent nets will be very easy to make as tying the knots and knowing where to place them take only a little practice.

Using a nightline

If you remembered to put fish hooks and string in your survival kit, a nightline is an easily rigged method of catching fish. Place a long, stout sapling across a narrow spot in a stream about three feet above the water's surface. Tie six or seven hooked lines to it. Weight each line. (Stones can be used for this purpose.) Bait the hooks with a variety of bait—crickets, worms, tiny frogs, minnows or pieces of meat if you can spare some. That way you will be able to determine for future reference which bait or baits attract which fish. In the morning check the lines. If you have a fish or two, you are set for the day. If not, change the bait and try again.

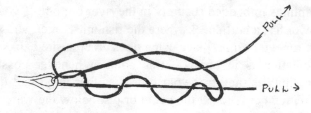

Attaching a fishing hook to a line.

Small fish (over two inches) make excellent bait. They can be kept alive by keeping them trapped in small pools. These pools are easily made by banking stones into a sort of corral on a quiet edge of the stream. Place your captured small fish within until needed. You can either use the small fish as an entire bait or cut strips if you feel the minnows are too big for the fish in your stream. Either method gets results as a rule.

Making a fishing spear

A spear is an excellent tool and will solve some of your food problems if you can locate a stream where fair-sized fish swim in pools or eddies near the bank. A spear is easy to make. There are two methods.

Method one: A long, straight, light pole, a Y-shaped twig (no more than a quarter-inch thick) and string or sturdy grass as a binding are needed. The pole should be about six or seven feet long and a half-inch thick. The Y-shaped branch should be such that the two prongs are further apart than half an inch. This is very important (see diagram).

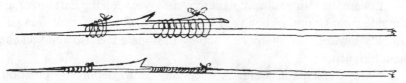

Two-piece fishing spear (top example shows tying procedure).

Trim your pole at one end so that a one-foot section of the top side is flat (see diagram). The point must be very sharp. The Y branch should be extremely thin as it is intended only as a barb to ensure your speared fish will not escape. Cut the Y branch so one prong of the Y is at least twelve inches long and the other part is only an inch or less. Using the string (or the sturdy grass) secure the long prong of the Y to the pole on the flattened top so the barb is four inches back from the point. This will allow the spear to pass through the fish and the barb to emerge on the proper side or to snag itself inside the fish.

The barb is not absolutely necessary, but without it the spear must be swung upward the instant the fish is hit to minimize its chances of escaping. An injured fish may escape but it will die shortly after and will be of no use to you. It is best to be sure, use the barb. (See diagrams of the various spears.)

Method two: This method requires only a pole about seven feet long that has a very thin branch about a foot from the bottom. Trim

Trimmed and sharpened one-piece spear.

that small branch down to form a sharply angled barb about an inch long. Sharpen the pole to a narrow, sharp end. This spear is neither quite as effective or as durable as the one in method one, but it is easier to make and requires no string or sturdy grass.

Making a gaff hook

A gaff can be made from a metal coat hanger if you have access to one. Simply straighten it out as well as you can, sharpen one end by pounding and grinding it with a heavy rock then bend the sharpened end until the rod looks like a shepherd's crook. Tie the other end securely to a sturdy pole and you are in business (see diagram).

Locate the fish you want to catch, slowly sweep the gaff along his far side from behind. When your hook is even with his fattest area pull quickly inward. The sharpened hook will impale the fish and you can haul him ashore.

Note: Remember, water is deceiving as to depth and position. Your fish may look closer than it really is. Allow for this or you will miss the spot and he will swim away. A little practice makes perfect.

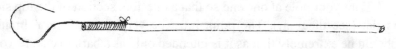

Gaff hook using a trimmed branch and heavy guage wire.

Summing up

With the above snares, traps, spears and nets you will be able to catch enough food to keep you going. The wise survivor concentrates on what is plentiful, so if there is a lot of fish depend on fish. Don't keep a run of snares if you have not caught anything after a few days. Retrieve them and utilize the wire to better advantage elsewhere. The old adage of try, try again does not always make good logic (remember LOGIC in the anagram?) in survival tactics. If at first you do not succeed, discard the idea and try something else. You can always go back to it later.

Conversely, if something does work well stick with it until it doesn't work any longer. A steady diet of anything may be tiresome but the alternative may well be worse. Survival has no patience for the fussy. Finicky is the privilege of the well-fed, pampered house cat and has no standing at all with the poor soul lost and alone in a less than friendly forest.

12 Locating Water and Determining Your Whereabouts

Water, Water Everywhere

Water, usually plentiful in any forest, is not always readily seen and can often be difficult to locate. You must be able to recognize the signs. If you are in mountainous or rocky country, check nearby cliffs and rock faces. Trickles of water exuding from rock indicate water. Often damp spots also indicate water. Use a sturdy rock to chip away where the trickle begins. You may be able to encourage a flow of water, enough at least for a drink or you might leave a container to catch a usable amount.

The dew that collects overnight on the blades of tall grass can be used in a pinch. Get out at first light and strip the dew from the blades by running each blade between your index and middle fingers. Lick the water off your fingers. It takes time but you will get an adequate drink from even a small field (five or six house lots) of grass.

Collect rainwater. The easiest way to do this is to leave an empty tin in an open space. Permanent containers can be fashioned by chipping shallow basins in rocks located in exposed places where rain will become trapped. Cover the basins when they are filled, otherwise the water will quickly evaporate.

Logs make poor containers as they are porous. This is mentioned because carving "bowls" in freshly felled logs has been tried and found generally unsatisfactory.

In the wilds, because there is no human habitation or industry to cause pollution, the water from falls, fast-flowing streams and rivers can be used in complete confidence. Creeks flowing over rocks produce good, aerated water. In still water (sloughs and swamps) boil **all** water before use. A good rule is: if you are uncertain of water always boil it—peace of mind is important to the lost person.

Clear water bubbling from underground springs is always safe. If you are fortunate enough to find such a spring, mark it well so you do not lose its location. This is the best water you will ever drink—and it will be safe beyond any doubt.

Lakes, large ponds and slow-flowing rivers present a problem. Watch for beavers. If you see these animals, or their dams, be sure to boil the water before drinking. The reason for this is an illness, called *Giardia*, that is caused by a parasite carried by beavers. Campers by the hundreds, if not thousands, have found out about *Giardia* the hard way over the years and they usually have access to medical help. The lost survivor does not have help and I know of no natural cure for this affliction.

Beavers expel the *Giardia* parasite into the water where it flourishes. *Giardia* will cause a bowel inflammation, severe pain and an intense bout of diarrhea that nobody needs. The only method of killing the parasite is through boiling the water prior to use. If there are beavers in the vicinity play it safe and boil the water.

Water in still, open or shallow places can also be poisonous because of alkaline content. Alkaline water usually has a strong smell of sulphur or other acrid odor. Avoid water that has an unpleasant odor or appears stagnant. If there are animal skeletons or carcasses in the immediate area you must assume the water is the culprit. Take careful note of the ground surrounding all pools. If the ground has a flaky white, gray or yellow consistency, the water is most certainly alkaline. Alkali, even a small amount, can do fearsome damage to the human neurological system ranging from brain-damaging seizures to death. These pools are common in desert areas, and although rare in forested and mountainous areas they are quite common in the flatlands of mountain valleys.

Snow and ice provide excellent water so look in the shadowed crevices of mountains. Even in the prime of summer a sharp eye can often spot a miniature glacier tucked away deep in the north side of a mountain crevice. Watch for these as you reconnoiter your area. Chip away the ice and allow it to melt. Do not eat ice and snow as is, it will harm your throat and may cause problems.

If the worst comes to the worst and you can find no water at all do not hesitate to drink your own urine. Sounds revolting, doesn't it!

Well, be that as it may, urine will cause you no harm and may well save your life.

First, the facts of the matter. According to urologists and physiologists the drinking of one's own urine, a practice fairly common in Asian countries, cannot possibly cause harm. Urine is 95 percent water and 5 percent urea, urea being the residue of the proteins your body breaks down during its normal daily routine. According to these experts urine contains no bacteria whatever, contains less germs than does saliva, your personal toothbrush, a cold meat or tuna salad sandwich. It contains trace amounts of about 200 minerals which your body needs. These traces include calcium, magnesium and potassium, all necessities of life.

Also, it is readily available as the average human produces about two quarts each day. Lives have been saved, especially in deserts, through its use by lost persons who decided that life was worth holding onto. While the entire subject sounds repulsive, life is far more important than squeamish reaction. So, if you are really strapped, use your urine. As the subtitle notes, water is everywhere.

Animals as Guides to Water and Other Goodies

Small aircraft tend to go down miles from the course the pilot recorded on his flight plan. That is why searchers so often find nothing and abandon the mission after ten days. They have simply been looking in the wrong place. That is little consolation to the lost individual, but it is one more cruel fact of a survivor's immediate life.

It is merely another reason why the stranded individual must face the possibility that his ordeal may continue for many weeks if not months. Because of this fact the survivor should learn to use animals as aids to survival.

Animals are excellent guides to the nearest water hole. Find their trails then keep a close watch on them. Large animals generally water at dawn and dusk. They all know where the water is and will, unknowingly of course, lead you to it.

Raccoons are extremely fine guides as they prefer to wash their food and will carry it to a favorite watering hole before eating it. Unfortunately, they are nocturnal creatures so in order to see them you will either have to go out into the moonlight (not recommended) or get up before dawn to catch a glimpse of them returning from the watering place. The best way is to find their tracks during the day, and then backtrack the trail. This applies to all animals.

It is a good idea to find out where raccoons find their water for another reason: besides water, it might supply you with another food source. Raccoons spend much of their time at streams feeding on small crustaceans called crayfish (some Americans call them crawdads and some Canadians call them prairie shrimp). These little crustaceans live near the shores of creeks, streams, rivers and lakes throughout North America. Crayfish are small, grayish white creatures. They resemble shrimp in a vague way (they are not at all pretty) and skitter around close to shore. They grow anywhere from half an inch to three inches in length (bigger in the deep south). The larger ones will provide a good food source (at least two dozen are needed for a worthwhile meal), and the smaller ones are good as bait for large fish such as jacks, pikes and other white fish. Crayfish should always be boiled. So watch the raccoons.

If you see a moose you can almost bet a lake is nearby—and a lake means cattails, bulrushes and lily-pads, three great food sources. Should you spot elk grazing it is likely you have found a field of useable plants such as sedum. If you see a cougar rolling around happily in a patch of weeds acting like a house cat you have found a catnip patch. Harvest a bunch of the leaves, making sure the cougar has departed, of course. Catnip makes a soothing tea which has medicinal benefits.

Hopelessly Lost? Find an Animal

Besides indicating water and food sources, animals will also tell you where you are—in very general terms. If, for instance, you have no idea of where you are, watch for animals. If you see a skunk with white spots instead of the familiar stripes on its back you are on the westerly side of the Rocky Mountains. The spotted skunk is seen in B.C., Idaho and some western mountain areas of Montana. The common or striped skunk (*Mephistis*) lives throughout the continent.

If you spot a large herd of buffalo wandering aimlessly through the bush you are probably in northern Alberta, namely somewhere in

Woods Buffalo National Park, the largest game reserve in North America. It covers such a vast area (17,300 square miles) that rescue may take days, weeks or months so prepare for a long stay. You could also be in Yellowstone National Park (3,458 square miles) of course, but the chances are you will know whether you were traveling in Canada or the U.S.A. These are about the only places in North America where sizeable herds of buffalo still roam in the wild.

Kodiak bears, the largest of the brown bear family (*Ursadae carnivore*), inhabit Alaska, the Yukon and the far northern reaches of British Columbia. Grizzly bears (*Ursus horribilus*) are a slightly smaller version of the kodiak. They are seen in the mountains and forests of B.C., areas of Montana and in Idaho. Oregon and Washington are also home to these beasts although in lesser numbers.

Kodiaks and grizzlies, like all bears including the small ones, are extremely vicious and always unpredictable. But they are a good gauge to your general location within a larger area. **Avoid all bears at all times**.

Mountain sheep are prolific in the Rockies as are mountain goats. Both are shaggy, usually white animals which walk and run balanced precariously on narrow rock outcroppings. They generally are in small herds.

Antelopes will tell you that you are in southern Alberta, southern Saskatchewan or northern Montana. They look like small deer but have two prongs instead of antlers and bounce when they run.

If you are on an open plain observe the small animals. Gophers, badgers, prairie dogs and jackrabbits will identify the area as the prairie regions of western Canada and the plains of the United States.

Jackrabbits are not your average bunny cottontail. They are quite large, achieve good speed in long hops and inhabit most prairie regions of North America. Their numbers increase and decrease during seven-year cycles.

Gophers are bigger than chipmunks, tan to brownish in color and live as separate families in burrows although a hundred families will inhabit a single field. Gophers seldom travel far from the den.

Prairie dogs (they look like large gophers) will tell you your location is south of the 49th parallel. They live in colonies of mounded burrows which are easily identifiable by their numbers and height. A prairie dog colony can cover several acres. Like their gopher cousins, they stay close to home.

Badgers (*Mustelidae taxidea*) are solitary animals. They are low slung and run hugging the ground. Badgers are dark brown in color with light stripes along their back. Their claws are formidable and they live in burrows underground.

All the above prairie animals are edible as emergency food but are not gourmet fare by any stretch of the imagination with the exception of the jackrabbit (a rifle or shotgun is needed to get one). The others can be caught with snares, but leave badgers alone as they are ferocious when cornered or wounded.

None of the above prairie animals will help you find water as they do not rely on creeks, lakes or rivers for their water as do larger animals.

A knowledge of specific animal tracks can be a tremendous help to a lost person getting a grip on where he is at the moment. Check the pages at the back with the drawings of animal tracks, they will help you identify the types of animals which will be sharing your surroundings with you.

13 Preparation and Cooking of Food

Cooking food in the bush is never easy and preserving it is equally difficult. Boiling or open-fire roasting is best because both methods are thorough and fairly quick. Cooked meat keeps well for several days under average conditions. It is not a good idea to keep raw meat for later use. If you were astute enough to prepare a survival kit, half the battle is won because you will have the three coffee tins to use as boiling pots. Unfortunately, few survivors have such foresight and end up with nothing to use as utensils. But wait! All is not lost.

A flat rock about nine inches in diameter and an eighth of an inch thick will serve well as a frying pan while a shallow hole in the ground makes a perfect oven/steamer. With both you can vary your menu and keep up your health as well.

The in-ground oven/steamer

An in-ground oven/steamer is a hole in the ground. It takes time to construct, but in the long run it can be well worth the effort. It must be about eighteen inches deep and a foot or so in diameter. It can be dug in the round or be square, but round is best because, for some reason, it distributes heat better.

Dig the hole, smooth the sides and tightly place several small rocks on the bottom forming a sort of dish. This will be your firebed. Where will you will find rocks? Rocks are everywhere in North America including deserts and are never hard to find so you can be fussy in your selection. Granitelike rocks are best as they get hot quickly and retain heat longer than "soft" rocks such as sandstone. Around the edges of your base, place layers of rocks one atop another until the pit's sides are rock-lined. Pound them into the sides of the hole to make them hold firm. Your pit should end up with a diameter of about eight inches.

About halfway up the inside of the pit, allow four or five rocks to jut out a couple of inches. These will serve as a support upon which your oven rack will rest.

You are now ready for a fire. (If you do not have matches see Chapter 16.) The best way to prepare the fire is to start a small blaze with very dry kindling or the wool from the dry tops of last year's cattails. When the fire is going well add small, dry branches. When the blaze is really good toss on a large number of hardwood branches (oak, maple, walnut are best) in small pieces, about five inches in length. Use enough to fill the fire pit to an inch or two below the stone supports. Feed the fire wood until it is very hot and the flames begin to subside. The wood will now be glowing hot. Lower a flat rock into the pit so it sits across the four or five support rocks. This is your oven rack. Be careful lowering it as by now the rocks will be starting to heat up.

If you have caught a larger animal—say a porcupine, raccoon or if you have some deer meat—you will have already prepared it by gutting the animal and skinning it (see below). Cut deer into portions of about two pounds. If the meat is a rabbit, raccoon or porcupine, cut it into pieces as you would a chicken.

Place the meat on the flat rock and cover the pit with a large, flat rock leaving about an inch of space along one edge for ventilation. Leave it alone for two hours and the meat will be well cooked by the time you remove the rock.

Another method is to place the meat in the pit and build the fire on top. It is not as good a cooking method as this cooking process takes longer. However, if you pack the meat in clay and leave it for several hours just beneath the very hot fire, it will be fine.

If you want to use the oven as a steamer, build the fire on top of the pit after placing your food on the oven rack with a covering of plenty of **wet** moss. This is a good method if you are lost near the ocean where you can find lots of seaweed or kelp. Place fish on soaking wet moss or in a bed of seaweed, cover the pit and leave it alone for an hour or so. This is mainly for situations where you have fish. Clams can be steamed but other shellfish should always be plunged into boiling water. Do not use the steam method to cook meat. The steam turns meat into an unappetizing, pale glob.

The best time to use an oven pit is when you intend to be away from your camp for a few hours. If you have not been rescued within ten days you should begin branching out in search of a road, railway track, trapper's cabin or even a high hill on which to erect a signal of sorts. This may mean you will be away from camp for a stretch of time. It is always better to return to a hot meal than to have to prepare something when you get back tired and disappointed.

Preparing meat

The preparation of meat is all important. Skinning an animal is not difficult if you have a knife, but can be tricky if you must depend on a sharpened stone (see Chapter 16). Prevent meat from coming into contact with the fur. This is important as letting the fur touch the meat in many cases will cause contamination. Food poisoning, always a high risk, is to be avoided at all costs.

If you have killed a large animal such as a deer, you must first "bleed" it. This should be done because as the animal cools, the blood solidifies in the arteries and makes the meat taste strong. Bleeding should be done within a few minutes, fifteen at the most. One way to do this is to place it so its head is much lower than its body (placing it on a sharp incline is one method). Cut its throat—a deep slash across the jugular vein—to allow the blood to flow freely. Then "gut" the animal by cutting its soft underside open from the throat to the pelvis. Because bears must always be considered a threat, bury the intestines and whatever else you do not keep. If you are by a lake you can safely toss the viscera into it as the fish will get rid of it. The fish will then stay around a day or two giving you a good chance to catch some of them. You may skin the animal where it is caught or wait until you get it back to your campsite.

Whether you remove the hide first or not, divide your kill into four pieces for easier transportation through the bush to your camp. This is called "quartering." Using your hatchet separate the two shoulder sections and the two hind quarter sections from the spine. A deer, if it is small enough, can be carried intact for quartering at the campsite.

An easy way to cart the animal is to build a triangular sled from three saplings. Take two saplings of five or six feet in length and tie them together near the top. The third sapling is tied crosswise at a point just below the middle. The finished product is in the shape of a letter A. Secure the meat on the cross-tie section. Drag the A-frame by hauling it from the narrow top. It is much easier than trying to carry the pieces across your shoulders. More than one trip may be necessary depending on size and weight.

Once you get to your camp, after you have skinned them, secure the quarters high up from the ground on branches a good distance from your lean-to. This will keep the meat—and you—safe from scavenging animals. By securing the quarters to branches, scavengers will be unable to reach the meat, although if they see it they will try. Use branches which can support only the weight of your meat and a squirrel. Do not interfere with or try to chase scavengers away. Just wait patiently until they tire and leave on their own accord. Allow the meat to hang for a day or two before cooking it. Hung meat becomes tender after a few days, very fresh meat is tough and tasteless.

Skinning the animal is time consuming but easy enough. You will know where to cut as between the hide and the meat is a thin layer of fat. Run your blade between the layer of fat and the hide while pulling upwards and back. Once you get moving it becomes a continuous operation. The legs will give you problems but this can be avoided by removing the legs at the knee joints. Save the hooves as they make good scrapers. Antlers make good digging utensils and excellent spear ends. Small bones and sinew serve well as needles and thread for sewing (see Chapter 16).

Keep the hide—you will need it if you are still in the bush come winter. You will have to prepare it carefully by scraping away all the fat and meat. Use the deer's hooves (or a rock with a sharp edge) as a scraper. This will take time as the hide must be completely free of fat and meat—absolutely free. Once this is done, s-t-r-e-t-c-h the skin between two saplings where the skin will "cure" in the sun over a period of a few days. The skin will provide you with a warm, but somewhat smelly, covering should you remain unrescued when winter comes. It will also provide a good flap for your lean-to opening.

Skinning small animals is only slightly different than skinning larger ones. Porcupines, obviously, must be handled very carefully. Their quills are barbed and, should any pierce your hands or arms, are not only painful but will fester if not properly removed. Forget the nonsense about porcupines shooting their quills. They do not.

Porcupines are easy to kill. They have been rightly called the survivor's best friend because they are such timid animals. If cornered they hunch into a ball. The quills, because they are so loose, fall out from the animal's frightened shaking and this is where the story that they shoot them originated. With a stout stick, flip the porcupine on its back. In this helpless state it is easy prey. Club it on the head.

Skinning a porcupine is tricky as you must avoid the quills. Keep it on its back as there are no quills on its soft underside. Cut it open, gut it and skin it. Bury the remains.

Raccoons are skinned the same way. Rabbits are "peeled" because once you have an edge to hold, the skin peels back easily. The same occurs with squirrels (also catfish among the fish family). Keep all animal skins—except porcupine—including those of the squirrels you snare. Sewn together they will make a good, warm hat and warm mitts. Now you know why you saved those tiny bones (needles) and the sinew (thread).

The best ways to cook your food

Cook squirrels and other small animals and birds in stews. They are too small to roast but simmered in water with tuber roots they make a good stew. Rabbit, raccoon and porcupine taste best when roasted on a spit or on a flat rock over the open fire. Keep the wood hot and the flame down. Support the spit across the fire with two sturdy Y-shaped branches and turn it continuously so the spit doesn't burn. The meat will take only an hour or so to cook if the fire is hot. Spruce hens should be cooked the same way.

Do not toss away the bones—or the fat—of your cooked animals. Boiled with wild onions, water-lily tubers and cattail stalks in a tin or pot of boiling water they make a good soup, a ready source of protein, minerals and vitamins. Such soup will keep for a day or two under normal circumstances.

Teas can be boiled in quantity and kept over a couple of days for easy-reach consumption. Keeping precooked food and teas available is a good idea in case heavy rainfall prevents the use of a cooking fire. The following foods and teas are recommended: boil white birch bark in a pot of water and keep the liquid handy. Each day drink six to eight ounces of this tea. It is full of vitamin C and for a survivor this is necessary to ward off scurvy. Labrador tea should also be kept on hand. It is also full of vitamin C. When brewed, if you have a little salt to put in it, the taste (with a little imagination) is similar to chicken soup. Labrador tea is described in the chapter on plants.

Vegetables and plants

You can munch on certain raw plants for a good snack between meals. These quick-snack plants are described in the chapter on plants. There are several wild vegetables which are edible when cooked but which you must not eat raw (see Chapter 5).

Nuts and some berries make a handy snack. Never eat wild berries unless you know what they are. Wild strawberries, raspberries, blackberries, brambleberries and blueberries are all well known to most people and all are good for you. So are buffalo berries, Saskatoon berries and red currents. However, **most** smooth, red berries are sour and may cause stomach pains while others are poison. Many black berries cause similar discomfort. **If you do not know the berry by sight—or are uncertain—leave it alone. Pay no attention to the old tale that if the birds eat them so can you**. Remember, birds' digestive systems are totally different from humans' systems. The recommended berries are described in Chapter 5.

Be **extremely** wary of swamp plants and ignore those you cannot identify readily. Hemlock and water hemlock abound in North America in swamps and in still water along shores of most lakes. Stay clear of swamps as there is very little food that can be gained from them. Stick to what you know—bulrushes, cattails and water-lily bulbs.

Unless you are an expert on mushrooms, avoid them. Puff balls are edible as are the so-called button mushrooms which will sprout up following a heavy rain. Puff balls that look like large table-tennis balls (some will grow to the size of basketballs) are alright. Open carefully as a puff ball may emit a powdery cloud. **Do not let the powder get into your eyes**—it will irritate them.

Puff balls are pink inside. Button mushrooms have a rounded, smooth top about an inch in diameter, are white on the outside, and are pink or light beige underside. Morel mushrooms, conical and mottled brown in color, are edible. Any of these three mushrooms can be added to a stew or eaten alone.

Unless you positively identify the above mushrooms **leave them alone**. Many mushrooms, such as the deadly nightshade, are poison while others cause hallucinations. The last thing you want is to become delirious and/or poisoned.

Toadstools are good for absolutely nothing. Not only are nearly all highly poisonous they are usually so ugly it is surprising that anyone would eat one—but many have. Many toadstools are shaped like an inverted cone while several types look like an umbrella blown outward by the wind. Many are scaly and nearly all are black underside. A great many ooze a black liquid.

Stay clear of any fungi seen growing under roots, on the bark of trees or growing close to a tree. The only fungi of this type that are edible are the elusive shiitake mushroom and the truffle, both so rare that they are not worth looking for. Fungi usually appear as thin semi-circles, are brown or black and often mottled. Unless you know for certain that you have unearthed a crop of truffles leave fungi alone.

For pictures of plants see p. 65–79. The poisonous plants are well marked and it is wise to learn them.

14 The Howling Arctic

The Arctic is one of the most inhospitable environments in the world. In winter its harsh climate is second only to Antarctica. It is a huge expanse of geography made more unfriendly by the lack of trees which would normally serve as shelter. Survival in the Arctic, even during the short summer months, is extremely difficult. Those who live there, who know the land and possess the proper equipment for the environment do not find life easy. During the long winter, survival is a terrible ordeal even when the survivor is well equipped; and it is almost impossible for anyone who finds himself with little to work with. Remember the key word is almost. Survival under the particular circumstances presented by the Arctic requires a level head and full utilization of what you have with you.

Anyone contemplating a flight over the Arctic in a private aircraft—regardless of the time of year—is advised to travel prepared even if the plane is the most modern type and the pilot is experienced. Wear the warmest clothing available and wear warm, lined, sturdy leather boots. Bring fleece-lined mittens even in summer. Pack a couple of heavy blankets in your suitcase. They will come in handy in case of trouble.

The survivor **must** remember above all else that the Arctic is a desert and the skills of desert survival apply. During the winter, instead of sand you will encounter endless miles of snow, numbing cold instead of blistering heat, and precious little to eat. Water is no problem but you need a good deal of snow to make a quart of water. The ratio is about 10:1 which means that ten tins packed with snow will melt down to about one good drink of water. The only good news is that there is no shortage of snow, but it should be melted otherwise it can hurt your throat with a sort of frost-bite.

During the four months of summer this desert is an endless tract of tundra. The Arctic is quite accommodating in summer, but the difficulties will still be hard to overcome. The water, as in a desert, is under the ground. Tundra remains frozen all summer from a depth of about two feet. Dig away the top layer and you will find all the water you need in the form of ice.

Food is more plentiful in the Arctic than in a southern desert. The Arctic is home to caribou, polar bears, musk-ox, arctic fox, snowshoe rabbits, fish, seals, ptarmigan and lemmings. The animals, however, are not teeming; and hunting them is a tedious business. Forget about hunting a polar bear—he will do you in long before you get him. Avoid polar bears at all costs and remember—polar bears do not hibernate. Musk-ox are equally forgettable because in order to catch one you have to take on the entire herd. Unless you have a high-powered rifle, e.g., a 30-30, 32-30, .35 or larger, you are not going to bring down a musk-ox.

Your best bet is to snare small animals, catch fish and make tea from moss and lichen (both good sources of vitamin C). During summer there will be adequate berries and green plants. The usual precautions described in the chapter on plants apply. With any luck you will be able to keep going until a nomadic band of Inuit (or a patrolling mountie) crosses your path. They are your best hope so watch diligently and hope one of these friendly and always helpful people finds you. But don't wait around for them. The Arctic is a huge expanse and travelers are few.

Making a shelter is the primary concern. In winter ideally you would build an igloo but such a venture is out of the question for any inexperienced person. However, regardless of whether it is winter or summer, a crude shelter can be constructed providing you have some-thing with which to cut into hard-packed snow or tundra. An ax, hatchet or large knife will suffice. Dig down about a foot into the hard-packed snow or the tundra. Bank the snow or sod above your digging so it forms four walls. This will serve as a windbreak. Light a fire for warmth and huddle inside. In winter, if you cannot light a fire, burrow into the snow as deeply as possible. This sounds cold—and it is—but really is not all that bad. Eventually your body heat will melt a sort of air space around you which will provide some insulation. Huskies have been doing this for centuries and they have survived very nicely. This is only good if you are dressed in Arctic clothing, such as a parka, etc.

Except during the summer months when plants are fairly plentiful, the survivor should rely mainly on lichen and moss. The best are reindeer moss, Icelandic moss and rock tripe (see Chapter 5).

Small animals are always scarce. They are there, but are very hard to see. The best way to spot them is to concentrate on one area until something eventually moves. Then you will know their grounds and snares can be set. All Arctic animals and birds are edible and none are of a poisonous nature. There are no snakes in the Arctic, so you really have to worry only about polar bears. Keep alert also for the ravens. The Arctic raven is a scavaging predator. They look like big crows but are meaner. Although they will never attack anything healthy, if they realize you are in a state of extreme weakness or unconscious these large, vicious birds will come at you. A flock of ravens make vultures seem like a flock of canaries. Arctic ravens can rip an animal carcass apart easily; a human body is unlikely to cause them any problem at all.

There is really little that can be said about survival in the Arctic. If you are well equipped you will have a reasonable chance; but if you have little or nothing the chances are very, very slim indeed. The best advice to anyone traveling into or flying over the Arctic is simple: be well prepared for any emergency every time you venture into this inhospitable land.

15 Get to Know Your Neighbors

Just like moving into a tough section of an unfamiliar city it is important when you are lost in the woods—indeed it is imperative—that you learn something of your neighbors. You must remember that you are dealing with wild animals and therefore you must determine what they are. Forest creatures are naturally curious so it is a safe bet they will be taking a good look at you. It is a good idea to determine what is watching you for the simple reason that one or more beasties could be considering you as the main course in their next meal.

The main problem is that you will not likely see the animals first. Wild animals are by nature timid and normally will go out of their way to avoid trouble; but bears are less timid than others and wolverines have absolutely no fear at all. Even the ferocious kodiak will keep his distance until he makes a decision on whether or not you pose a threat or are just passing through. Bears, however, are notorious for snap decisions.

The animals to be most wary of are the carnivores—bears, cougars, wolverines and wolves. Neither a cougar nor a wolf is likely to attack a human unless the animal is cornered, wounded, rabid, extremely hungry or startled. Mostly cougars and wolves will run. Cougars are somewhat unpredictable, however.

Bears of any size, even the so-called cinnamon bear, are dangerous. (Cinnamon bears are small black bears that have developed a brownish coat. They are seen more in Northern Ontario than anywhere else.) Any sign of weakness, illness or outright fear helps a bear decide on how he will deal with those who intrude into his territory. Of course, if a bear is startled reaction will be quick. A bear will respond by remaining still and waiting for you to move, turning and running or becoming aggressive. Your reaction will determine its course of action. Therefore, it is important to know if you are sharing the woods with bears.

The wolverine is a totally different piece of goods. Wolverines are the largest member of the weasel (*Mustela*) family, a group collectively famed for offensive traits. The wolverine is without doubt the most obnoxious of the family. It is not a very large animal. A wolverine will normally weigh between thirty and fifty pounds.

It is also known in various regions as "skunk bear," a name derived from appearance and smell. Two pale brown stripes which run the length of its dark brown body and its obscenely foul smell remind people of a skunk (the two are only distantly related) plus it displays a resemblance to a miniature bear. In some areas it is called, quite wrongly, a polecat, actually another name for a skunk.

Wolverines are the homicidal psychopaths of the animal world—a small, furry version of *Tyrannosaurus rex*. Fearing neither man nor beast, wolverines are without doubt, pound for pound, the most savage animals alive. They are known to have attacked grizzly bears. An authenticated case on record in the Yukon archives, relates how a wolverine attacked a mature grizzly, tearing open the bear's jugular vein in its vicious attack. The bear grasped the wolverine in his huge claws as he fought back. Then, weakened from the loss of blood, the bear fell to the ground still hugging the wolverine in a death grip. In so doing he pinned the smaller animal under his great bulk. Helpless under the dead bear, unable to move or work his way free the wolverine also perished. The bear's carcass, still relatively fresh, was discovered by two patrolling Department of Fish and Game wardens. When it was rolled over for inspection the dead wolverine was discovered, his jaws still clamped on the bear's throat.

Because a wolverine is both hunter and scavenger it matters not a whit to him whether his food source is dead or alive—if it isn't dead he will happily kill it. For that reason alone you must be especially wary of this beast. Also, you must take steps to protect any meat you might capture for later use by securing it from a high branch.

A wolverine moves at three speeds: its walk is really a fast trot; its lope is a fast canter and at full speed it moves as a blur. A wolverine is a perpetual motion machine. Even when eating he moves in small circles never still for a minute. It will occasionally stop and stand upright in one spot to test the wind. Even then its head moves continuously and furtively from side to side, always alert. Fortunately, wolverines are not overly commonplace. With any luck at all you will never encounter this animal.

Cougars (*Felis concolor*) are also called panthers, mountain lions, pumas and catamounts. Males, measuring about seven or eight feet long, and females (slightly smaller) are solitary, mostly nocturnal animals. On occasion a pair will travel together. Kittens remain in the lair, dependent upon their mother, for many months and are quite large before being allowed to venture outside. The coloring of an adult ranges from tawny brown to an almost violet-gray shade.

In the manner of all cats, cougars move stealthily and silently. They are very fast for short sprints so don't try to outrun one. Like any cat, a cougar is aloof and will not likely bother you unless you bother it. Cougars who have attacked humans have usually been those who have come into built-up areas. Those in the wilds are generally too timid to have anything to do with humans. An adolescent cougar will attack people if it has been orphaned before it learned to hunt while an adult cougar will attack if it is too old to hunt or is sick, injured, rabid or cornered.

If you are lost in cougar country you will hear them—a loud scream in the dead of night that will scare you out of your socks—but you will likely never see one. They will not approach or enter a campsite under normal circumstances. Knowing they are in the vicinity, and avoiding them, is the only real precaution you need.

Bears must **never** be trusted. Should you sight a bear leave the immediate area at once. Never run but do leave quickly and as quietly as you arrived. Remember always that a bear runs faster than you and he will outdistance you easily. He can swim faster and climb higher than you. Do not try to outrun, outswim or outclimb a bear. If he sees you he will probably watch to see how you react. Back slowly away making no undue or sudden moves. Keep moving until he is out of sight. Only then should you move faster. Be certain never to move between a mother and her cub(s) for she will attack without a second thought and will give no warning whatever.

There is very little defense against a bear. Their huge claws and power are far superior to anything an unarmed man or woman has to offer. The best defense is avoidance. If you are attacked probably the best thing to do is fall flat on your face, cover your head and neck and lie as still as you would if you were dead. If luck is with you the bear will go away. However, you will probably be in for a mauling regardless of what it finally decides to do. (Apparently foresters in B.C. are now carrying mace sprays for use against bears; it is reported to work well.)

It is possible to share a fishing stream with a bear providing you keep downwind a distance and never appear as a threat. It is best to go to the opposite bank downwind. Watch him closely in case he decides to move your way. In that case leave at once.

Bears will not hesitate to rob your camp if you leave anything lying around that might tempt them. Suppose, for instance, that you discover a bee hive and manage to scoop some honeycomb and then leave it lying loose. You may well acquire a bear as your houseguest. The same thing applies for berries, meat and fresh game. Leave nothing edible lying around. Remember always the basic rules of survival, particularly the **itemize** rule, which admonishes you to keep everything and keep it in its proper place.

Wolves travel in packs because they are family-oriented animals, although they will travel in pairs. They are also the victims of bad press. The old stories about wolves are for the most part complete nonsense. Old-time authors such as Jack London spun very exciting yarns about wolves using a time-worn scenario familiar to wolf stories: glowing red eyes pierce the darkness of the night as a pack of these ferocious beasts, howling a savage oratorio to the moon above, surround a trapper's campsite. They begin circling slowly, moving ever closer. Occasionally the sharp report of the trapper's Winchester .30-30 breaks the stillness of the northern night and another wolf falls. But there is only one trapper and there are many wolves. The pack circles, patiently closing the distance until, in a fierce, snarling rush they attack.

This type of narrative sold a lot of books but it never once happened in real life. Wolves in the wild are timid animals and have never been known to attack a trapper's campsite—or any human for that matter. As a member of the Royal Canadian Mounted Police who patrolled the Yukon for many years was quoted as saying: "Any man who tells you he was attacked and eaten by wolves is a damn liar."

Usually the worst thing wolves do when a human intrudes into their territory is to frighten him with a serenade of yapping and howling which lasts throughout the night. Many people believe this is the wolves' way of telling the person to clear out. Personally, I think this belief is pure conjecture, another old trappers' tale. From my observations, wolves howl every night for a number of reasons including invitations to potential mates. It is the nature of wolves to howl and it is not likely the serenade is intended for human benefit at all.

However, if one assumes the old tale is true, when the traveler leaves the next morning—as trappers and patrolling mounties generally do—the wolves figure the fellow was scared away; if the intruder stays—as lost persons should—the wolves will accept him as just another minor annoyance. Wolves are the least of your worries.

Fire is a true deterrent to any wild animal. Keep your fire going during the night. You won't need a large one. Also good is the smell of urine. Urinate all around the perimeter of your campsite, against trees, rocks and bushes. Keep it active.

I cannot personally vouch for this next method (in fact, I don't believe it) but several woodsmen of my acquaintance swear it works. If you have any empty shell casings, scatter them here and there around the perimeter of your campsite. Wild animals, my friends insist, do not like the smell of gunpowder.

Summing up

Study the pages of animal tracks (spoor) at the back of this book in order to be able to recognize the tracks you will see along the way. Much of the battle in wilderness survival is knowledge of spoor. You will learn from tracks because you will see more spoor than you will animals. Tracks tell you which animals are in the area. Sometimes you will be able to determine how long ago the animal passed and they always point the direction he was heading. Also, they will give you a rough idea of how many animals are in the immediate area. Animal tracks and other animal signs can also lead you to water and other useful items.

16 He Who Has Nothing

This chapter is not meant to chide those who blunder into misadventure totally unprepared although, heaven knows, they deserve a stiff dressing down. This chapter is directed to them in the hopes that it might help, despite their carelessness. It is also written for those who had a kit but lost it through one reason or another. Even the best kit can be lost if a canoe overturns, or it burns following an aircraft crash or its owner drops it when he stumbles into a chasm. Mishaps happen.

Finding yourself with absolutely nothing, though reason to worry, is no reason to panic. Whether you realize it or not, even in this darkest of moments you will possess an item or two which will help keep you alive. Your shoe laces and your belt will become part of an impromptu kit and your shirt or T-shirt can serve as a bandage or a tie for a splint. Check the trees around you. The bark of cedar trees will be of use (the Pacific Native Indians made clothing from cedar bark), as will supple branches of some bushes. Stones provide cutting utensils and flat rocks easily turn into cooking utensils.

The basic rules of survival still prevail. You must see to a proper shelter without delay. This can be done quickly enough by following the directions in Chapter 3 utilizing fallen saplings as poles. Or, if you are in a forest with small, close-growing trees, say eight to twelve feet tall, bend four of them in toward each other. Tie them near the top with strips of bark, woven strands of coarse grass or your belt. Tear boughs from fir trees to make walls placing the boughs atop each other as you would on a lean-to.

Another method is to tie (with grass rope, thistle twine or bark strips) a crossbar (a fallen sapling) across two upright trees. Bend smaller trees downward so they slip into place under the crossbar so they cannot snap back into position. These will act as slope poles. Tear boughs from fir trees and place across the slope poles as on an ordinary lean-to. Make walls and a floor the same way.

If you must cut down a tree or three you will require an ax of some sort. How do you manage the construction of an ax from nothing? The first thing you do is find a sharp-edged rock or stone of reasonable size. Ideally, it will be oval to almost triangular. These shapes are best for purposes of creating an ax. Smaller stones can also be fashioned into various tools of sorts.

Take the best large stone with the sharpest edge you can find. Choose an edge of at least six inches. If you can find flint, so much the better. Sharpen the stone further by striking it on both sides along its widest edge in a downward motion with a smaller rock until it is as sharp as possible. Then locate a stout branch from a hardwood tree. Ideally, it will be about fifteen inches in length and have a diameter of about three inches. This is where your boot laces come in. Secure the rock to the stoutest end of the wood using the laces to tie it. Tie the lace in the cross-over method. If you can, split the end of the branch far enough back so it can be pried apart enough to form something of a wedge to hold the rock. It will be stronger and much better. Tie the rock into the wood and finish the tie by securing the split end.

This ax, a primitive tomahawk, will be sturdy enough that, with careful use, it will cut a small to medium tree deeply enough for you to break it loose. Remember, the cutting time will be a great deal longer than normal. If you can't find a suitable handle use the ax by holding it firmly in your hands to chop at the tree. It will eventually chip away enough for you to fell it. Take heart from the fact that beavers have been cutting trees for countless centuries using only their teeth. The rock utilizes the same procedure—more or less.

No string, rope or laces? There are several types of plants that grow long, slender grasslike leaves which, when braided together, make a sturdy rope. Use cattails or burr reeds for best results although almost any type of coarse wild grass will serve the purpose. Using three or four strands braid them together by crossing each over, under and between the others. Your first attempts will be very discouraging but keep at it. After several tries you will become reasonably proficient. (If you get really good at weaving you will be well advised to weave a carrying basket). Any number of ropes can be produced easily and quickly. Use these "ropes" to lash saplings and branches, etc., together in the construction of your lean-to, back-pack and whatever else you can make out of such material.

With sharp stones you can manufacture both cooking and eating utensils from stone or wood. First, find a flat rock of porous material.

As with everything else, stones and rocks have varying degrees of hardness. Soapstone, which is easily chipped, is ideal. It must be long and wide enough to cover the fire area when sitting on stones which you will set out to act as feet. It must also be thick enough that a bowl can be formed in it. Chip away at the center until a shallow well is formed then chip outward toward the edges. It should be hollowed sufficiently to hold at least a pint of liquid. This is extremely tedious work and must be started on your first or second day when you still have the energy for such endeavors. Be careful not to allow stone chips to get near your face or eyes. Make your chipping motion away from yourself and turn the stone as you chip.

Once your cooking utensil is complete, turn your attention to an eating dish. Wood is adequate. The principle is the same. Find a burl (a hard knot) of wood—or cut one from a medium-sized branch. To begin with your piece of wood (the burl) should be about six inches across (more or less) and about three inches deep. With a sharp rock dig out the center to a depth of two inches. Then whittle away toward the outside edges in a circular pattern. If you keep some roundness to your bowl, finishing it will be easier.

When you have a suitable bowl carved find an abrasive rock. Any stone with a rough surface will do. Rub the sides and bottom of the bowl until it is as smooth as possible. You now have a suitable bowl which will double as a drinking cup.

The making of a stone pot and a wooden bowl is a tedious project but the work serves some very important purposes: (1) it provides you with two pieces of survival gear you didn't have before, (2) the work is a morale booster in that it takes your mind away from your troubles for a time, and (3) it proves to you that you can take charge of your own destiny, and that there is no reason why you cannot eventually get out of the woods by contributing to your own rescue.

As soon as possible get busy with another project of great importance: the making of a utility knife. Again you must look for a suitable stone. Locate a flat piece of shale or flintlike stone about ten inches long, four to five inches wide and a half-inch thick. Use the edge of a second flat stone to chip the rock into a rectangle approximately three inches wide.

Chip along one edge from one end a length of six inches. As you chip, fashion the blade so it will have a point. Once the edge is flattened repeat the process along the other edge. Now, in a lengthwise motion from wide end to the point, using the coarsest stone you can find, hone both edges until they are as sharp as possible. You will produce a crude knife with a double-edged blade about six inches long and three inches wide, with a rough, four-inch handle. Depending upon how sharp you can make it, your knife will cut rope and can be used to dig out deep-set vegetable roots. It can also serve as a skinning knife. Such a knife will pare tubers and soft roots but, because it is unlikely to be sharp enough, it will not cut with great finesse.

These three projects will consume at least three days of your time, and maybe even four; but you are lost and not immediately going anywhere so you might as well do something constructive. Take heart in the knowledge that your primal ancestors started out under roughly the same circumstances and they managed to do alright. And, of course, they didn't have this book to guide them along the way.

How to light a fire from nothing

Lighting a fire without matches is nowhere near as easy as the promotional pamphlets and films about the Boy Scouts may have led you to believe. As a matter of fact it is a tedious operation and can prove difficult. Scoutmasters never admit it, but they all employ little tricks and gimmicks (a few concealed matches or a touch of lighter fluid, not usually available to anyone lost in the woods) that make it all look easy. After all, they are trying to convince impressionable little boys that life in the bush is great fun. But we know better, don't we?

Coaxing a flame into life using a clump of dried cattail cotton or a little pile of dry tinder and a flint is difficult and time consuming. There is also the art of obtaining a flame by rubbing two sticks together. Success lies mainly in the quality of the materials used and a vast reservoir of persistence.

The materials needed for a successful fire from nothing require careful selection and deserve further mention. In the absence of matches you will need a lighting agent plus tinder, kindling and logs. Let us consider first the lighting agents: flint is a hard, marble-white stone with a thousand uses, one of which is the production of sparks that will ignite tinder—eventually. If you are not sure that the stone you have found is flint, strike it against a second stone. Flint will readily produce sparks. Few other stones will.

Two dry sticks can also produce fire through a process known as "friction" but "fiction" is a more apt description. Choose sticks of hardwood (maple or oak) for best results. Spruce, fir or balsam as well as deciduous softwoods such as poplar, catalpa and willow can be used but they will take much longer to ignite.

If you have a pair of glasses (or a thick glass of any sort) the lenses may be useful as a lighting agent as, if thick enough, they **might** produce a pinpoint of sunlight as a magnifying glass will.

For tinder use **very dry** moss, cattail wool or dried grass. Make a small, loose pile for best results. Have small, **very dry** twigs handy to place on the fire when the first flames appear. For kindling use small, narrow shavings or chips of dry wood from the inner part of a fallen tree and place on the fire after the tinder has established a reasonable flame. Keep the first flames small as that will give the fire a chance to establish itself. If you pile the heavy wood on too soon all you will get is smoke and the flame will die.

For fire logs and other fuel use only the driest wood available, preferably split branches with the bark still attached. Use hardwood as the heat is steadier and hotter. Trees of the evergreen species are generally so full of pitch that they smoke, snap and throw sparks which can cause troubles. Wet wood of any type produces a lot of smoke and will not burn successfully. A dead tree can be a good source of fuel—and it is easy to harvest. However, because such wood is often rotten and spongey it may burn poorly.

If you are near a bog, look for peat (dry only) as a block of dried peat will smoulder for hours and will produce excellent heat. In mountain country look for coal which sometimes appears in outcroppings. A few chunks of coal will keep a fire fueled a long time.

We now come to the part where you must start the fire. You will find that it is no easy task regardless of whatever you have read in the Boy Scouts' manual.

Starting the fire with flint

This will actually work, however slow it may be. Prepare your fire area by clearing away debris and old leaves. Pull out all the grass in the fire area so it will not cause a secondary fire which might spread outward. If it is very dry use it as tinder. In the center of the area pile a small, loose mound of the driest moss, cattail wool or grass you can find. Holding a piece of flint firmly in one hand, **well inside** the moss, strike the flint with a second piece. Keep striking until the sparks catch enough to cause a small glow at the base of the moss. Put the stones aside and blow very, very gently on the spot where the glow is evident.

Eventually, the moss will puff into a small flame. You must now fan the flame, still gently, until it spreads to a greater part of the moss. At this point place a few twigs on the moss, continuing to blow if necessary; and when these begin to burn put some of the kindling on in the shape of a tent. When the flames are sufficient you can introduce the logs singly, small ones first.

If you have a pistol, shot gun or rifle, the shells can be used to advantage. A shot gun shell is easily opened. Uncrimp the paper end, remove the flat stopper and empty out the shot (BBs). (Save the BBs. Tied in a small piece of cloth they are useful as weights for fishing lines.) Open a rifle or pistol cartridge by carefully twisting the slug until it comes free of its crimped edge. Remove all wadding and pour the black powder carefully **under** the tinder and **near** the center. This is to avoid burns which will occur if the igniting powder catches your fingers (which should be at the edge) too close to the flash point. Toss any empty casings near the perimeter of your camp-site. There is a theory afoot that maintains that wild animals react fearfully to the smell of gun powder. It is probably worth a try.

If you arrived at your predicament through a plane or motor boat mishap perhaps you will be able to salvage some gasoline from the tank. Place a small amount of gas at the center of the tinder pile as an aid to starting the fire. Use gasoline every bit as sparingly as you would gun powder—and certainly with the same caution.

There are a couple of ways to start the fire with friction (with or without gasoline or gun powder).

Method One: for this you will need two pieces of dry wood as described above and an interminable deal of patience. Of the several methods used possibly the most widely publicized is the one where a piece of flat wood, scored with a deep groove, is placed inside the dry tinder. Then a vertical stick held between the palms of the hand is rotated with great vigor. The theory behind this is that after a time the end of the stick heats the board to ignition heat, the moss will catch fire and gentle fanning can commence.

This method works but usually expends a colossal amount of time and energy. Use only if all else fails. In most cases the palms of your hands will heat up long before the wood and you will develop blisters which you certainly do not need.

Method Two: while an equally slow procedure, it will work most of the time, but prepare yourself a long stay. Fire is produced through the use of two very dry sticks. Hold a stick in each hand and place the end of one stick into the tinder. Rub the stick vigorously and steadily with the other stick near the end until the tinder puffs into a small flame. At that point the rules of fanning apply. This stick against stick method works neither easily nor very well but is better than the first.

Using glass as a magnifier: this will only work on bright, sunny days. If you have a piece of thick, clear glass experiment to determine if it will act as a magnifying glass. Sometimes thick eye glasses will serve the purpose. Position the glass very close to the tinder and adjust the angle of the glass to catch the sun's rays. You will have to try various angles but, eventually, if a tiny pinpoint of light about the size of a sharpened pencil end appears against the tinder you might be in business. Hold the pinpoint on **one** spot until it begins to glow into the beginning of a tiny flame. Blow gently on the spot until the flame widens. Gentle fanning will produce the rest.

Once you get a fire going it is in your best interest to keep it burning. It is easier to get up a couple of times during the night to stoke the fire than face the necessity of rubbing two sticks together or striking flints every day. The chances are you won't sleep for the first few nights anyway, so you might as well watch the fire.

Summing up

It would be nice to be able to offer more encouragement to those who end up in the bush with nothing to work with, but all that can be said is stick with the task at hand and hope for the best. If you search diligently you will find enough berries and roots to keep you alive even without utensils to cook them. Stay with the plants described in Chapter 5 that need little or no cooking, conserve your energy, keep the fire going and think up ways to utilize what you have. You will be surprised what you can do with nothing. You just have to work harder at it than if you had remembered to pack a survival kit.

17 Signaling for Help

Most rescue attempts utilize aircraft and helicopters at one point in the rescue effort. For that reason it is wise to produce some sort of message which can be easily seen from the air. Tall sticks implanted into the ground about ten feet apart with a bright cloth tied to each one can catch the attention of overhead viewers. The most practical message is a simple SOS with an arrow pointing in the direction of your camp. The aircraft crew will then be able to direct ground searchers to the proper direction and those on the ground will not be required to travel any further than necessary to get to you.

For an SOS to be seen from the air the letters must be wide and lengthy, be placed in a cleared space and must contrast with the surroundings. There is little sense in using brown logs on a field of brown grass—they will not be seen from the air in all likelihood. Green pine branches, on the other hand, will work just fine. In some cases just trampling the grass into the letters will work temporarily. The trampling has to be done every day as the grass bounces back quickly.

If you are the victim of a plane crash use whatever material you can salvage from the plane. Bright fabric from the seats is good as are carpets and head linings. Cut the material into long strips or secure a series of short strips together. Form your SOS with these strips in an open clear space, peg or weight them down and leave them there.

Check your SOS every morning and repair or replace any part that needs it. The letters should never be less than ten feet long by three feet wide and always as colorful as possible. Surprisingly, trampled snow shows quite plainly from the air. If you are lost in winter you simply have to tramp out SOS and an arrow in very wide, very large letters right into the snow in an open field.

If you are near a lake (and have the necessary materials) make a raft, secure your SOS material on the raft and anchor it off shore where it will be visible from the air. If the lake has a sandy beach, tramp out

SOS and the arrow in the sand. Bright stones or rocks laid in the letters help to enhance the contrast.

There are many variations and any one will work on any given day. The important thing is to make your SOS big enough and to always add the arrow pointing in the direction of your campsite. Thus, by making a few signals in various clearings, you have added an important ally to your cause. Don't be reluctant to make several signals in several areas. **Always** remember the arrows.

Keep small piles of fir brush prepared in clearings close to your camp and at the first sound of a low-flying aircraft light them. The smoke may attract some welcome attention.

Use your flashlight to signal any aircraft you see—even high flying liners not looking for you. Someone may be looking out and might see the signal. You never know. Flashlights work best before dawn and after dusk. A glass mirror or piece of metal work well on sunny days as reflective signals. Always flash the letters SOS in morse code. The code letters are three short flashes, three long flashes and three more short flashes. SOS is commonly referred to as dot dot dot, dash dash dash, dot dot dot (...---...). Flash this series of signals many times separating each series by about five seconds. Continue flashing until the pilot either acknowledges (usually by dipping the wings) or the plane disappears. If the aircraft is a helicopter the pilot will probably acknowledge the signal by hovering over you. He may then depart, but don't worry as someone will be coming to get you shortly. If the helicopter is an air force search and rescue craft someone will in all probability be lowered to you.

Once you know for certain that rescue is a sure thing you can begin to think about dismantling your camp, but do not start until the rescuers actually arrive because you may not be taken out right away. For any number of reasons, such as inclement weather, the rescuers may decide to delay departure.

You should always take out the equipment with which you went in. Leave nothing lying around that could harm a roving or curious animal. Gather up remaining food and all other garbage and either burn or bury it. Retrieve and dismantle all snares and traps. Take in your fish nets and nightlines. Leave your lean-to intact and place inside it the nets, spears, implements, dishes and other utensils you have made. You never know when these items may assist someone else. Make absolutely certain the fire is extinguished before you leave.

18 Odds and Ends

Bush survival is not so complex that every segment requires its own chapter. First aid is for instance a short subject because there are severe limitations on what you can do either for yourself or anyone who happens to be with you. Wounds, cuts and abrasions must be treated with what is at hand whether it be a clean cloth, a thickness of spiders' webs or plantain leaves. Sprained wrists and ankles are best treated by immobilizing the injured area for as long as possible. Broken arms and legs must be set then immobilized.

Immobilization of a broken arm or leg is best attained through splinting the limb after setting the break as well as you can. Splints can be made easily by using branches on both sides of the break, secure them with twine, cloth strips, adhesive tape or ropes woven from grass or dry nettles. Immobilize a broken arm by using a sling which will keep the arm tight against the chest so the hand rests just below the breastbone (sternum).

Keep all wounds clean and covered until they scab over. Change bandages or plantain leaves often. Wash out used cloths so they can be reused.

Certain plants and trees produce salves and medicines and the ones which might help you are mentioned in earlier chapters. In areas of B.C., Washington, Oregon and northern California a tree called the cascara grows. It can be used as a source of medicine for the treatment of constipation, which can become a real problem in the woods. Cascara trees are usually found with alders, maples and birches. They will grow twenty to forty feet high and six inches in diameter, but in very poor sites they are often reduced to a shrubby bush. Leaves are green, measure two to seven inches long and are about one to two-and a-half inches wide. They are finely toothed and have a blunt end, are round at the base and are hairy underside. In June, yellow-green flowers appear in clusters along twigs. Later a black, round fruit appears. The bark is thin, gray-brown, smooth and grows scaly with age. The bark produces an excellent laxative. Used sparingly, it can help a survivor keep regular bowel habits as constipation can be every bit as troublesome as diarrhea. Both are treatable with plants and herbs.

Make use of the bones from animals you snare. When sharpened they make good needles. Strips of animal hide, thinly cut, produce good thread for patching torn cloth and leather.

***

The following recipe sounds revolting but the result is not bad tasting. A thick, nutritious soup can be made by boiling a pot full of nettles and/or cattail cores. Throw in a few hundred ants and a few dozen minnows (heads and all) and simmer for an hour or two. How to catch ants? Take one of your coffee tins, dissolve some sugar or sweet liquid from a flower or plant in a quarter inch of water on the bottom, tilt the tin at a sharp angle against an ant hill and wait. The ants will enter the tin to get the sweet whatever-it-is. They will fall into the water and you've got them. Minnows? Scoop out a shallow corral at the shoreline of a nearby stream or lake where small fish are in abundance. By diverting some of the flow into the corral you will gather up enough minnows to use in your soup. A little herding might be needed to induce the minnows into the corral. Keep the surplus alive for bait in case you decide to fish with the hooks you were told to include in your basic kit.

Another excellent recipe is for a stew which can be made from squirrels and thistles. You will be surprised at how good it tastes and it is full of nutrients. Skin and gut the squirrels caught in your snares, remove head and feet and simmer with the thistles. Thicken with seeds from pigweed (if available) or pollen from cattails or bulrushes. Toss in a few wild onions or some water-lily tubers for added taste.

You might turn up your nose at such recipes now but after ten days in the bush, long after your cookies and powdered orange juice have run out, the above-mentioned dishes will be gourmet fare. Usually the first thing a stranded survivor discovers about himself is that he is no longer the fussy eater he once was.

***

If you are lucky enough to discover a hive of bees you will be able to harvest some honeycomb providing you are careful about it. First of all, the hives of wild bees bear no resemblance to hives of domestic bees. They usually look more like a disorganized mass of gray paper and sometimes they are nothing more than a huge honeycomb stuck inside a hollow tree.

They are often anchored under rocks, inside the pulpy remains of long-fallen trees or in the branches of standing trees. They are easy enough to spot as the humming and constant coming and going of thousands of bees is hard to miss. The noise alone can be frightening. Make sure the hive belongs to bees and not wasps. Hornet and wasp hives usually hang like gray bags from branches or rocky overhangs. Besides, there is really no resemblance between bees and wasps. Bees are smaller than wasps and hang around flowers. Wasps and hornets lurk around barky trees, shrubs and other places where insects, their natural foods, nest.

Light a small fire under the hive an hour before dusk. That is the best time as the bees will be retiring for the night and won't be flying randomly about. You do not require a big flame; your interest is in smoke. Make a great deal of thick smoke—as much and as thick as you can manage—and direct it right at the hive. Smoke puts any bee to sleep without harming it permanently. Most of the bees will fall to the ground as they try to flee the hive. They will not harm you in any way unless you pick them up. Open the hive very carefully and extract a reasonable amount of honeycomb. There will likely be bees attached so shake them loose. Leave immediately. When the bees revive they will repair the nest and carry on as if nothing happened.

Warning: This operation is not for the faint of heart or for anyone who can't exercise extreme patience and caution. Bees are nothing to fool with. Make sure your smoke is thick and that the hive is totally immobilized before you open it. Even one half-awake bee will fight to the death in defense of the hive. Follow the rules and the reward will be worth the effort.

***

After you have given up hope of being found you must think of walking out on your own. But wait at least fourteen days before undertaking what may well prove to be a dangerous adventure. Prepare for the trek with great care by stockpiling roots and plants to eat along the way plus a cooked animal or two. If you have some honeycomb bring it along as a high-energy food. Start early in the morning—just after dawn—and walk five or six hours each day. Stop no later than 3:00 P.M. No watch? Keep an eye on the sun.

In summer the sun will set in the west about 70° from due south; in spring and autumn the set will be approximately 45° to 50° from due south. In the dead of winter the sun sets about 30° from due south. Using those figures you can figure out where the sun should be around 3:00 P.M. In the high Arctic summer, of course, the summer sun never actually sets, while in winter it never fully rises. The above figures, therefore, have no value north of the boreal tree line.

Be very certain to blaze your trail. This is very important if you are to avoid walking in circles. Walking in circles is one of the easier things to do in a thick bush or forest as well as being the least productive of ventures.

When the afternoon begins to wane, stop for the day and settle in for the night in order to conserve your strength. It will mean building another lean-to, of course, but it is necessary. Besides, now you know how to do it so it will be quicker to set up. Use the remaining light to find water and some cattails or other edible plants.

If you stumble upon a road or a railway track follow it—and stick faithfully to it—because roads and tracks **always** go somewhere. Roads and tracks usually head north and south or east and west. The smart survivor will always head south or west as those two directions are more likely to lead you to civilization.

You will have no trouble determining if roads or tracks are active or abandoned. If weeds grow undisturbed all over the road or wheel ruts are filled with dust, or if tall weeds grow between and crawler weeds grow across the tracks you are on an abandoned stretch. Do not despair, though, as both still go somewhere. Sooner or later you will come to a settlement of some sort, a town or perhaps a farm. It might be a ghost town or a deserted farm, a logging or mining camp either active or deserted, but at least it will afford some shelter. The chances are good that it will have a few inhabitants. Once you find even one person, your troubles should be over.

A word of warning about walking out: do not even **think** about walking out until you are very certain the search has been called off unless you have already discovered the road or the tracks. A person in one place is always easier to find than someone who is wandering aimlessly around. Moreover, if you walk strictly on the tracks or road you will also be easier to spot.

As you walk keep an eagle eye open for good stopping spots. If, by noon, you find an ideal place to set up camp stop there and then. Travel under the old cliche that says a bird in the hand is worth two in the bush. Ideal places to camp are usually few and far between. If you pass on one at noon there is a good chance that you will not find another that day. If the site is extremely favorable do not be reluctant to spend two or even three days there. Someone passing overhead in a plane may well spot your signals. Play the survival game intelligently. Use logic and common sense and your chances for rescue are very good. Be imprudent or reckless and you probably won't make it out.

***

The survivor, of necessity, must become his own weather forecaster, a easy to master ability, and helpful because it benefits one to know what the following day is likely to bring. During spells of pleasant weather when the skies are clear the only thing to worry about is that you know it can't last—good weather never does. The trick is to know more or less when the weather will change so you can be prepared.

The old adage "Red sky at night, sailor's delight; red sky in the morning, sailor take warning," holds true for the most part. The Pacific Coast Natives told the legend that Sin, the sky god, disguised as a red hummingbird, would fly across the sky to inform his mother, Fair Weather Woman, of his wishes. If Sin appeared in the evening the following morning Fair Weather Woman would release breezes which would bring good weather. If Sin appeared at dawn, however, she would withhold the breezes and the day would be stormy.

On clear nights take a look at the moon. If it shines clear and bright, the next day will be fair. If it appears circled with faintly colored rings of orange, red, purple and yellow—much like those of a rainbow—your weather is about to change with rain or snow falling within a day or two. (These halos are sometimes referred to as moon rings, dog rings or moon dogs.) If you don't have a good source of water, now is the time to make ready your water tins. Set them in cleared spots in order to collect rainfall.

Rain is also foretold by the leaves of deciduous trees such as elm, poplar and other green leaf bushes. The shiny side of leaves turn inward so the dull underside will show a few hours prior to the start of rain.

Pay heed to crickets if they have been active in your area during the nights. So long as their chirps are loud and rapid, the weather will remain fair. As the chirping begins to slow, so also is the weather changing. If, on a cloudy evening, crickets suddenly fall silent hustle into your lean-to. The rain will start within minutes.

Watch the birds. If they suddenly cease flying and fall silent it will be for one of two reasons: there is either a heavy storm about to begin or there is a falcon in the area. Either will silence the birds and hurry them back to their nests. You will learn to spot the difference.

If you have planned some activity which will take you a distance from your camp check the sky. If the sky is overcast with dark clouds it is wise to postpone the venture. If it is something that must be done, do not stay longer than absolutely necessary. If a heavy wind suddenly begins, head for home quickly as that is a final indicator of an impending storm. Try to get back before the wind falls to an ominous silence as that period of time is the proverbial calm before the storm. Once the wind dies you will be drenched in a downpour within minutes if you have failed to have scurried back into your shelter.

It is a good idea for anyone who travels through or flies over densely forested, sparsely inhabited areas on a constant basis to learn as much as he can about wilderness survival. There are many excellent books available on the subject of plants which can be used for food and medicines. Your local camping supply store may offer seminars—perhaps extensive courses—on the art of bush survival. A few survival schools are available in certain parts of North America. These usually advertise in outdoor magazines and are generally worth their fee.

Many years ago the Royal Canadian Air Force operated a survival school in which, under stringent and realistic conditions, many hundreds of flying personnel were trained to survive in the bush. Following seven days of classroom instruction the students, in groups of twenty to thirty, were dropped off in a forest, bush, desert or tundra with a couple of instructors. Some were paired off while others were assigned a single role. From there, for two long weeks, they learned the ways of survival first hand. The average student lost about ten pounds during the fourteen days in the bush—but he learned how to survive. Not all passed the final tests (there are many reasons why men fail such tests) but all emerged safely. Those who didn't make it were offered a second course at a later date. Most gratefully accepted.

The school's unofficial motto pretty well summed up the spirit of those who challenged the strict and difficult course. The motto "down but not out" can be adopted by anyone who ends up lost and alone in the wilds of North America. Whether the venue is a forest, dense bush, a desert or the Arctic there are really no valid reasons why anyone cannot survive a stint as a survivor. Most of those who do not survive fail because they first lose their heads and then lose their grip on reality.

It is sincerely hoped you never have to use this little book in deadly earnest. But, since you have read it, perhaps you have gained something from it, found it educational and perhaps even entertaining to some degree. Remember—many people have survived the ordeal of being lost in the bush so there is no reason why you should fail.

Animal Tracks

Front   Rear

Bear
Grizzly: Front 5½"; Rear 10"
Black: Front 3¾"; Rear 7"
Alaskan & Polar: Front 10½"; Rear 6"

 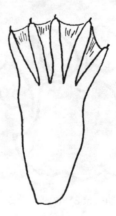

Front 3"   Rear 7"

Beaver

Front 1⅓" long

Rear 1¾" long

Bobcat

Front 3" x 3½"

Rear 3" x 3"

Cougar

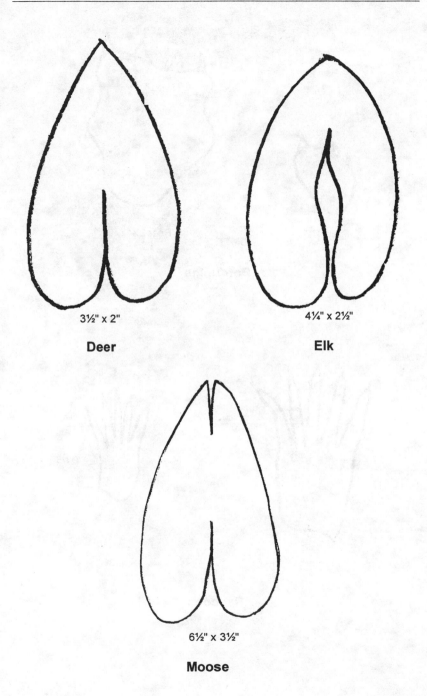

3½" x 2"

Deer

4¼" x 2½"

Elk

6½" x 3½"

Moose

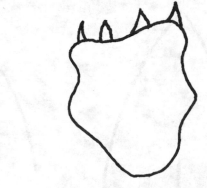

Front 1¼"   Rear 2½"

Porcupine

Front 3¾"   Rear 3¾"

Raccoon

Front 2¼"   Rear 2¼"

Squirrel (in snow)

4" long; 3" wide   5" long; 4" wide

Wolf   **Wolverine**